PAUL'S SUMMONS TO MESSIANIC LIFE

INSURRECTIONS: CRITICAL STUDIES IN RELIGION, POLITICS, AND CULTURE

INSURRECTIONS: CRITICAL STUDIES IN RELIGION, POLITICS, AND CULTURE
Slavoj Žižek, Clayton Crockett, Creston Davis, Jeffrey W. Robbins, Editors

The intersection of religion, politics, and culture is one of the most discussed areas in theory today. It also has the deepest and most wide-ranging impact on the world. Insurrections: Critical Studies in Religion, Politics, and Culture will bring the tools of philosophy and critical theory to the political implications of the religious turn. The series will address a range of religious traditions and political viewpoints in the United States, Europe, and other parts of the world. Without advocating any specific religious or theological stance, the series aims nonetheless to be faithful to the radical emancipatory potential of religion.

For a complete list of books in the series, see pages 129–130.

PAUL'S SUMMONS TO MESSIANIC LIFE

Political Theology and the Coming Awakening

L. L. WELBORN

Columbia University Press NEW YORK

COLUMBIA UNIVERSITY PRESS
Publishers Since 1893
NEW YORK   CHICHESTER, WEST SUSSEX
cup.columbia.edu
Copyright © 2015 Columbia University Press
All rights reserved

Library of Congress Cataloging-in-Publication Data

Welborn, L. L., 1953–
  Paul's summons to messianic life : political theology and the coming awakening /
L. L. Welborn.
    pages cm. — (Insurrections: critical studies in religion, politics, and culture)
  Includes bibliographical references and index.
  ISBN 978-0-231-17130-4 (cloth : alk. paper) — ISBN 978-0-231-17131-1 (pbk. : alk. paper) — ISBN 978-0-231-53915-9 (e-book)
  1. Bible. Epistles of Paul—Criticism, interpretation, etc. 2. Bible. Epistles of Paul—Theology. 3. Time—Religious aspects—Christianity. 4. History—Religious aspects—Christianity. 5. Agamben, Giorgio, 1942– . I. Title.

BS2650.52.W44 2015
227'.06—dc23

2014033472

Columbia University Press books are printed on permanent and durable acid-free paper.
This book is printed on paper with recycled content.
Printed in the United States of America

c 10 9 8 7 6 5 4 3 2 1
p 10 9 8 7 6 5 4 3 2 1

COVER DESIGN: ALEX CAMLIN
COVER IMAGE: *HEAD OF AN APOSTLE* BY PETER PAUL RUBENS © ALINARY ARCHIVES/CORBIS

References to websites (URLs) were accurate at the time of writing. Neither the author nor Columbia University Press is responsible for URLs that may have expired or changed since the manuscript was prepared.

For my sons, Locke and Mark, and for my rabbi, Bernard Barsky

Das kommende Erwachen steht wie das Holzpferd der Griechen im Troja des Traumes.

—Walter Benjamin, *Das Passagen-Werk*, Konvolut K

Owe no one anything, except to love one another; for the one who loves the other has fulfilled the law. For the commandment, "You shall not commit adultery, You shall not kill, You shall not steal, You shall not covet," and if there is any other commandment, it is recapitulated in this word: "You shall love your neighbor as yourself." Love does no wrong to the neighbor; therefore, love is the fulfillment of the law. And this knowing the *kairos*, that the hour has come already for you to awaken out of sleep, for now our salvation is nearer than when we first believed. The night is far advanced, the day is drawn near. Let us therefore cast off the works of darkness, and let us put on the armor of light. As in the day, let us conduct ourselves decently, not in revelries and drinking bouts, not in sexual excesses and debaucheries, not in quarreling and jealousy. But put on the Lord Jesus Messiah, and do not make provision for the flesh, toward desires.

—Romans 13:8–14

CONTENTS

PREFACE xi
ACKNOWLEDGMENTS xix

1 | NEIGHBOR (A) 1

2 | KAIROS (B) 11

3 | AWAKENING (C) 23

4 | AWAKENING (C') 37

5 | KAIROS (B') 45

6 | NEIGHBOR (A') 55

7 | CODA 71

NOTES 73
INDEX 127

PREFACE

IF THE IMPRESSION does not deceive, Paul's letters have acquired a new legibility in recent years. This is the case not only with respect to accessible writings, such as 1 Thessalonians and 1 Corinthians, letters determined by concrete situations, but also with respect to Paul's last and most visionary composition, the epistle to the Romans. That this is so is due not merely to advances in knowledge of the historical context, though these have been considerable, nor to the overcoming of anachronistic frameworks of interpretation imposed during the Reformation, though the new perspectives have been salutary, but to something deeper, something historic, something essential to the crisis of our time, of which Karl Barth already had the intuition. From somewhere, a flash of light has made the characters of Paul's ancient text legible, and is stirring hope.

The index of this phenomenon is the sudden preoccupation of a group of philosophers (Jacob Taubes, Alain Badiou, Giorgio Agamben, Slavoj Žižek, Kenneth Reinhard, Eric Santner), none of them Christian, several of them avowed Marxists, with the letters of Paul. Why should secular, indeed irreligious philosophers turn to the apostle Paul and find in him the embodiment of the figure of the "militant," a truer type than the figure of Lenin installed in the imagination of philosophers at the beginning of the twentieth century? Merely to raise this question is to penetrate to the core of the phenomenon of Paul's present legibility. For these philosophers may be said to be acutely aware of the threat that hangs over the present moment, a danger described variously as a "state of exception" or "biopolitics" by Agamben and as "the absolute sovereignty of capital's empty universality" by Badiou, but a danger upon whose dehumanizing consequences all are agreed. In a world where political processes are increasingly controlled by capital, and where social relations are mediated by images, there is the danger not only that the masses may become, as they always have become, the tools of the ruling class, but now, more seriously, that human sociality may be alienated from itself by the global triumph of a digital machine capable of manipulating perception and controlling memory through the invincible logic of the integer. The supreme danger is that the residue of the other, the neighbor, upon whose alien reality my own humanity depends, may be fully metabolized by the perpetual motion of capital, which homogenizes all identities. Or, to speak in the language of our tradition, the danger now exists that the Judeo-Christian sense of social obligation embodied in the commandment "You shall love your neighbor as yourself" will be entirely swept away by a resurgence of that structured inequality which was the basis of the political economy of the Roman Empire.

It is the sense of Paul as a contemporary to a perilous moment for humanity that has drawn the philosophers to the apostle and has given his texts their new legibility. Paul wrote his epistle to the Romans at the "midnight" of the first century, the reign of Nero. The sole sovereignty of the successors of Augustus was an ongoing "state of exception" in which politics perished, a new structure of power constituted and reconstituted by the imposition of various degrees of dependent subjecthood and, in the last instance, by terror. The wealth of the emperor and his syndicate depended upon the vigorous exploitation of the resources of the provinces and upon the enslavement of a significant portion of the population—the latter institution maintained by the cruelty of crucifixion. By the age of Nero, spectacle had become an all-encompassing feature of social experience, which not only blurred the boundary between the real and the representational, but threatened the expropriation of human sociality itself. The mass burials uncovered by archaeological excavations outside the gates of Rome are a grisly testimonial to the dehumanization of precisely that segment of the population from which Paul and other evangelists recruited the members of their messianic assemblies. The philosophers who, in a moment of danger, seek to link their present to the apostle's past have glimpsed in Paul's messianic faith a spark of hope.

For anyone familiar with this literature and its antecedents, it will already be clear that the hermeneutic which governs the new philosophical readings of Paul is that which Walter Benjamin gave to historical materialists in "On the Concept of History" and in some notes in his unfinished *Arcades Project*. In contrast to the method of historicism, which seeks, by forgetting the subsequent course of history, to lay hold of the eternal meaning of a work, and in contrast to the popular, liberal assumption that a work is susceptible of a variety of legitimate interpretations, depending upon the interpreter's perspective, Benjamin proposed that a work—a text such as Romans—contains a temporal index that connects it to a specific epoch, and that it comes forth to full legibility only for a person who is singled out by history at a moment of danger, a perilous moment like the one in which the work was composed. Whether Benjamin's hermeneutical principle applies to all literature, to every text, I am incompetent to judge. But this hermeneutic seems particularly appropriate to crisis literature, to texts such as Romans and the Gospel of Mark or the Apocalypse of John—works composed, as Benjamin would have it, "in the immediate messianic intensity of the heart." The new philosophical interpreters of Paul merit our attention because they have exposed themselves to the danger that threatens our world. In that respect, they are the readers for which Romans has been waiting.

Benjamin's hermeneutic will be presupposed in what follows. Only, of the two moments that this hermeneutic seeks to hold together in constellation, I will place the greater emphasis upon the earlier one—Paul's own *kairos*. This is not only because I am a New Testament historian by training, but also, and more importantly, because for all the light that has recently been cast upon Paul's letters, it does not seem to me that Paul's *kairos* has been fully disclosed. Therefore, the image that should be formed when the historian grasps the connection between the perilous moment in which he reads and the one in which Paul wrote remains obscure, has not fully crystalized. And thus, there has not been an explosion of consciousness as a result of the new encounter with Paul, no "now of recognizability," as Benjamin terms it, or, to employ Paul's own phrase, no "renewal of the mind" (Rom. 12:2).

I shall argue below that the defect in current philosophical interpretations of Paul is a consequence, in large measure, of the philosopher's commitment to the project of knowledge, a commitment that Paul did not share, and that, in fact, he vigorously opposed (1 Cor. 1:18–25). In particular, Paul did not believe that the *kairos* depended upon the self-presence of consciousness. Nor did Paul share the philosopher's passion for universal truth. Paul's truth, to the extent that he speaks of one, is a singularity. Crucially, the temporality that Paul posits as a creation of the messianic event stands opposed to every philosophical teleology; there is no room in Paul's "now time" for the future. I shall argue that Paul's concept of the "now time" can only be understood when it is located in proximity to Jesus's proclamation of the nearness of the kingdom of God. Finally, the political activity that Paul's faith demands has nothing of the passivity to which the philosopher seems resigned. Paul's fighting spirit seeks to hasten the awakening.

The most certain evidence that Paul's *kairos* has not yet been fully disclosed is the absence of two crucial paragraphs of Romans from the discussions of the philosophers. The absence is most notable and most puzzling in Agamben's commentary and in Badiou's monograph. Instead of Romans 13:8–14, the attention of philosophers has focused upon an earlier and provisional formulation of Paul's understanding of messianic time in 1 Corinthians 7:29–31. What is it that blocks access to Paul's most mature and intense formulation of the law of messianic life and the eschatological faith that empowers that life in Romans 13:8–14? Two obstacles may be clearly identified. First, the pernicious text of Romans 13:1–7, which, according to the traditional interpretation put forth by commentators, enjoins submission to the governing authorities instituted by God. With good reason, some interpreters question whether Romans 13:1–7 is authentically Pauline, and not rather a piece of Hellenistic-Jewish parenesis interpolated at a later date. I will devote scant attention to this problematic text here, choosing rather to expend my constructive energies upon the restoration of the neglected paragraphs of Romans 13:8–14 to the center of our concern. I will be content to have demonstrated that the political ethics demanded by Paul in Romans 13:8–14 is inconsistent with the traditional interpretation of Romans 13:1–7.

A second obstacle is the persistence of interpreters, both philosophical and traditional, in assuming that, to the end of his life, and even in his latest epistles, Paul was waiting for the so-called Second Coming of Jesus. As we shall see, Paul nowhere mentions the *parousia* in Romans (or in any of his later epistles). Instead, Paul summons believers to an "awakening" by grasping the full implications of a messianic event that had already occurred. I will argue below that Paul's eschatology underwent significant development from his first epistle (1 Thessalonians) to his last (Romans), and that this development had the character of an intensification: that is, the future hope of Paul's early years became, in the crucible of his suffering, a present reality. This is a crucial contribution to my dialogue with the philosophers, since even the best of Paul's philosophical interpreters are captive to the traditional notion that Paul decomposed the messianic event into two times—resurrection and *parousia*—and that Paul continued to await the Second Coming of Jesus at the end of time. I will argue below that those who are waiting for something to happen, even those who are waiting for the inevitable to happen, remain enthralled by the future, and so never enter with Paul into the "today of salvation."

In sum, the traditional interpretation of Romans 13:1–7 as a Pauline preachment of submission to the authorities and the conventional assumption that Paul's eschatology was static and that he continued to await the Second Coming are the two rams whose blood must fill the trench, if the spirit of Paul's most intense formulation of the demands and conditions of messianic life in Romans 13:8–14 is to rise and speak to us. I would suggest that, if either of these doctrines is sacrosanct, the reader should lay aside my little book and read no further.

Finally, it is my impression that Christians and non-Christians have, for the most part, despaired of our capacity for neighbor-love, especially if the neighbor embodies ethnic or religious differences or is an avowed enemy. So strongly are the populace and its perceptions molded by the hands of capital and its political servants. In this midnight of the twenty-first century, we must hold fast to the memory of Paul, who did not despair of glimpsing in the little groups of mainly oppressed persons who had joined his messianic assemblies the vanguard of the sons and daughters of God, who would awaken and take responsibility for the redemption of the world (Rom. 8:19).

ACKNOWLEDGMENTS

IT IS a joy to acknowledge the assistance of colleagues and friends who graciously read and commented on this book at various stages in its evolution. At the top of the list are three who alternately challenged, instructed, and inspired me: Ward Blanton, Brigitte Kahl, and Laura Nasrallah. Several others read the first draft of the manuscript and provided valuable criticism and advice: Dale Martin, Gerd Luedemann, Terrence Tilley, Ben Dunning, Neil Elliott, John Penniman, Yung Suk Kim, Deborah Wallace, and Gary Luttrell. Only after the manuscript was finalized did I think to send it to my former Fordham colleague Christophe Chalamet (now of the Université de Genève); Christophe's observations were so insightful that I wish I had contacted him when the work was still in genesis.

Many years ago (in the summer of 1979) in Freiburg, Lloyd Spencer (Leeds University) introduced me to the writings of Walter Benjamin. The consequences of that encounter are still working themselves out in my thought and in my life.

A partial précis of this book was presented as a paper at a symposium in honor of the retirement of Daniel Patte from the faculty of Vanderbilt University in April, 2013. I am grateful to the organizers and participants in this symposium for critical observations and encouragement to complete the manuscript.

I wish to express my sincere gratitude to the editors of *Insurrections*, Slavoj Žižek, Clayton Crockett, Creston Davis, and Jeffrey W. Robbins, for including my work in their series. Wendy Lochner, my editor at Columbia University Press, her assistant Christine Dunbar, and copyeditor Robert Demke, as well as the entire production staff, especially Anne McCoy and Kathryn Jorge, have been exemplary; without them, the book would be far less readable.

This book arose from a prolonged dialogue with the three people to whom it is dedicated: my sons, Locke and Mark, and my friend Bernard Barsky. Each challenged me to make the argument of the book more forthright and accessible. In many respects, this book is a continuation of the graduate seminar on Paul and the philosophers that I taught with Rabbi Barsky in the spring of 2007.

My beloved wife and partner of thirty years, Diane, listened to drafts of this book read aloud on the patio on long summer evenings and offered many helpful suggestions; she is my best and truest critic.

PAUL'S SUMMONS TO MESSIANIC LIFE

1 | **NEIGHBOR (A)**

IN ROMANS 13, Paul enlarges upon a conviction that he first expressed some years earlier in his epistle to the Galatians (5:14): "For the whole law is fulfilled in one word: 'You shall love your neighbor as yourself.'"[1] Leviticus 19:18 (Septuagint), from the heart of the Holiness Code,[2] is cited as warrant for the one obligation that remains for members of the messianic community: "Owe no one anything, except to love one another; for the one who loves the other has fulfilled the law" (Rom. 13:8). Epitomizing the Torah in a demi-Decalogue (Rom. 13:9),[3] Paul asserts that "the word" of Leviticus 19:18 "summarizes," or "recapitulates," all the commandments: "You shall love your neighbor as yourself." Thus, Paul is able to conclude that "love is the fulfillment of the law" (Rom. 13:10).

As is well known, such summaries of the whole law are found elsewhere in Jewish tradition. The "Golden Rule" is attributed to Rabbi Hillel as the essence of the Torah.[4] A generation after Paul, Rabbi Akiba cited Leviticus 19:18 as the principle that sums up and contains the whole of the Torah.[5] But the frequent citation of Leviticus 19:18 in early Christian literature[6] makes it likely that Paul took the quotation from the tradition of Jesus's sayings, as attested by Mark 12:31 and parallels.[7]

The conclusion that Paul is following a tradition established by Jesus gives point to the assertion of Jacob Taubes in his exposition of Paul's political theology: Paul's designation of neighbor-love as the fulfillment of the law represents a radical reduction within the primordial core of the Jesus tradition.[8] As Taubes observes, Paul cannot have failed to know that Jesus taught the dual commandment.[9] Asked by a lawyer "which commandment in the law is the greatest," Jesus answered, "You shall love the Lord your God with all your heart, and with all your soul, and with all your mind. This is the greatest and first commandment. And the second is like it: You shall love your neighbor as yourself. On these two commandments hang all the law and the prophets" (Matt. 22:35–40).[10] Paul's omission of the command to love God from his summary of the whole law in Romans 13 cannot, Taubes argued, be accidental, given its centrality in the Jesus tradition, but reflects Paul's conviction that this burden has been lifted from the shoulders of the new people of God, in consequence of the messianic event.[11] How this came about Paul explains in Romans 5: through divine *kenōsis*.[12] This is Paul's interpretation of the death of the Messiah for the weak, the ungodly, and enemies: "God commends his love toward us in that while we were still sinners the Messiah died for us" (Rom. 5:8; cf. Rom. 5:5–11).[13] For those who have experienced the messianic *klēsis* (calling), there is now only one imperative: to love the neighbor as oneself, that is, to love the nearest embodiment of the ones for whom the Messiah died, following the kenotic movement of divine love. Thus, the divine *kenōsis* has sublated the first commandment.

To his credit, Taubes did not shy away from the psycho-theological implications of Paul's sublation of the commandment to love God. By way of a series of lengthy citations from Freud's

Moses and Monotheism, Taubes reprises Freud's version of the history of religion: "Judaism had been a religion of the father; Christianity became a religion of the son. The old God the Father fell back behind Christ; Christ, the Son, took his place."[14] Taubes comments: "This is also a contribution to the problem of the dual commandment and its radicalization in the love command: the focus on the son, on the human being; the father is no longer included."[15] For Taubes, the assertion that God the Father has been dethroned is not an ontological claim, but a religious way of speaking about a psychological development. Paul's sublation of the commandment to "love God with all your heart and soul and might" lifted the burden of guilt imposed by paternal law. As Paul's spiritual "descendent,"[16] "Freud, so to speak, enters into the role of Paul" and tries to realize Paul's theological vision by a new therapeutic method.[17] "Freud . . . continues Paul's work by striving to liberate us from the burden imposed by the obscenely cruel paternal agency that we harbor within ourselves."[18]

Now, ironically, the sublation that, according to Taubes, was intended to transport Paul's readers beyond all superego inculpation, so that they might freely obligate themselves to mutual love, has the consequence of making the command to love the neighbor more difficult to fulfill, because it removes the force of the divine mandate. The importance of the divine mandate is inscribed in the tripartite structure of Leviticus 19:18: first, the prohibition—"You shall not take revenge or bear a grudge against any of your people"; then, the remedy—"You shall love your neighbor as yourself"; finally, the rationale—"I am the Lord" (Septuagint).[19] Without the divine mandate, it is scarcely possible to imagine that one could undertake something so unreasonable and difficult as loving the neighbor as oneself.

It is the difficulty of neighbor-love apart from the divine mandate that Kenneth Reinhard, Eric Santner, and Slavoj Žižek contemplate in their three inquiries into political theology as the legacy of Jacob Taubes.[20] The insuperable difficulty of the biblical injunction is vividly evoked in the introduction by way of the frighteningly realistic assessment of Freud in *Civilization and Its Discontents*: "Let us adopt a naïve attitude towards it," Freud proposes, "as though we were hearing it for the first time. We shall then be unable to suppress a feeling of surprise and bewilderment. Why would we do it? What good will it do us? But, above all, how shall we achieve it? How can it be possible?"[21] The commandment seems more unreasonable when the neighbor is a stranger: "If he is a stranger to me, and if he cannot attract me by any worth of his own that he may have acquired for my emotional life, it will be hard for me to love him. Indeed, I should be wrong to do so, for my love is valued by my own people as a sign of my preferring them, and it is an injustice to them, if I put a stranger on a par with them."[22] But if the neighbor happens to be an enemy, then the biblical injunction seems positively absurd: "I must confess that he has more claim to my hostility and even my hatred.... If it will do him any good, he has no hesitation in injuring me.... Indeed, he thinks nothing of jeering at me, insulting me, slandering me, and showing his superior power."[23] Freud concludes his reflections on the difficulty of neighbor-love by confronting the persistence in human beings of a fundamental inclination toward aggression, a primal mutual hostility. Freud observes that the neighbor is for us "too often only a potential source of cheap labor, someone to be tricked or exploited, a sexual object, someone who tempts us to satisfy our aggressiveness on him, to exploit his capacity for work without compensation, to use him or her sexually without consent, to seize his possessions, to humiliate him, to cause him pain, to torture and to kill him. *Homo homini lupus.*"[24]

Reinhard, Santner, and Žižek struggle mightily to discover resources for rethinking the biblical injunction to love the neighbor in a world where the divine throne is vacant. Reinhard takes up Lacan's proposal of an alternative logic for sexuation, not as a static situation, but as an event, an encounter involving a choice that is retroactively named either "man" or "woman."[25] The passage of the human through an indiscernible zone that Lacan called the "not-all" in the process of sexuation encourages Reinhard to seek for an analogous path beyond the friend/enemy dichotomy of politics. Reinhard finds the opening to this path in the figure of the neighbor, who emerges beyond the boundary of politics in the generic field of Humanity.[26] But in order to operationalize the decision to *love* the neighbor as oneself, Reinhard has recourse to Lacan's argument that a third love is necessary, the love of God, which is the model of symbolic love, the love of the father that sustains the symbolic order, even for those who are not believers.[27] Hence, even "the [Lacanian] subject loves the neighbor only by means of the love of God."[28] In the end, Reinhard escapes from the difficulty of Paul's sublation of the love of God by reverting to a psychoanalytic version of the dual commandment.

Santner endeavors to remain faithful to the commandment of neighbor-love in an era when historical materialism sets the parameters of discourse.[29] Santner combines the Lacanian theory of the constitution of the subject with Franz Rosenzweig's attempt to recover an experience of the miraculous in everyday life. Rehearsing the account of the primal scene that gives rise to unconscious formations in the infant subject by Jean Laplanche (a student of Lacan), Santner posits that the excess of parental desire which cannot be metabolized by the child through symbolization sinks into the unconscious as "residues."[30] These "residues" of the desire of the other constitute an "internal alien-ness, maintained, held in place, by external alien-ness."[31] A "miracle" for Santner would represent "the event of a genuine break in the fateful enchainment of unconscious transmissions," an opening of the subject toward the inner alien-ness of the other.[32] Santner grasps that the biblical commandment to love the neighbor "directs our minds, indeed our entire being, toward that which is most thing-like about the other."[33] But how can a genuine exodus occur from the deep patterns of enslavement to the needs of the self, so as to love the other? Santner concludes that to conceive of a kind of love that exceeds mere object cathexis "is already a mode of registering the region of being we call God," and "testifies to the ongoing necessity of theological thinking."[34] Thus, Santner endorses Rosenzweig's project of monotheism as "a form of therapy that allows for a genuine return to the midst of life with our neighbor."[35] Rosenzweig's own experience demonstrated that the "miraculous achievement" of neighbor-love "required some form of divine support—ultimately a form of *love*—kept alive, in turn, by a certain form of life."[36] Like Reinhard, Santner seeks to evade the difficulty of Paul's radical reduction of the dual commandment by offering a "postsecular" solution to the human predicament: monotheism as therapy.[37]

Žižek styles his contribution to the political theology of the neighbor not as a response to the problem identified by Taubes, but as "a challenge to the so-called ethical turn in contemporary thought, a turn often linked to the thought of Emmanuel Levinas."[38] Žižek targets what he takes to be the gentrification of the neighbor in the thought of Levinas, the neighbor as my mirror image, in whose human face I experience the epiphany of the transcendental Other who summons me to infinite ethical responsibility.[39] Against Levinas, Žižek insists that beneath the neighbor as my *semblant* there always lurks the unfathomable abyss of a monstrous Thing whose inhuman excess requires me to practice justice, or, as Žižek terms it, "ethical violence."[40] But just as Simon Magus is a cipher for Paul in the Pseudo-Clementine *Homilies*,[41] so Levinas is a mask for Paul in Žižek's essay. Žižek simply rejects the notion that Paul sublated the commandment to love God, insisting that "it is a mistake to oppose the Christian god of love to the Jewish god of cruel justice."[42] Žižek asserts that "Christianity merely assumes the Jewish contradiction" between "monotheistic violence" and "responsibility toward the other."[43] Thus Žižek hopes for the "return of the Jewish repressed within Christianity: the return of the figure of Jehovah, the cruel God of vengeful blind justice."[44] Žižek quotes illustratively the last song Johnny Cash recorded before his death, in which God is depicted as a kind of political informer who "comes around" "taking names," deciding who will be saved and who will be lost.[45] On the day-of-judgment to which Žižek looks forward, Christianity will once again become Judaism,[46] abolishing the illusion that Paul reduced the dual commandment.

I would like now to join this discussion about the difficulty of fidelity to the love command by returning to the origin of the problematic in Romans 13. Commentators generally recognize that the following paragraph in Romans 13:11–14, in which Paul reminds his readers of the *kairos* and summons them to an awakening, "provides the eschatological rationale for performing the ethic in the preceding pericope."[47] Yet, strangely, none of the philosophers who have wrestled with the implications of the Pauline reduction of the dual commandment has discussed the intensely eschatological text that follows in Romans 13:11–14. This omission is especially surprising in the commentary on Romans by Giorgio Agamben, since Agamben recognizes that the recovery of Paul as the fundamental messianic thinker in our tradition requires, above all, an understanding of the meaning of the time that Paul defines as *ho nun kairos* (the now time).[48] The omission is just as puzzling in the book on Paul by Alain Badiou, since Badiou has been most successful among our contemporaries in articulating in a secular idiom the meaning of the process by which a newly awakened self comes forth, in response to Paul's message of the resurrection.[49] Only old Jacob Taubes, in his Heidelberg seminar of 1987, called attention to Paul's "eschatological profession of faith" in Romans 13:11–14, and the concept of the "now time" contained within it, as the context for understanding Paul's revolutionary confidence in the fulfillment of the love command.[50] Unfortunately, the fact that "time was pressing so personally" upon Taubes, because of an incurable illness, rendered impossible an exposition of his insight into the relationship between the two pericopae in Romans.[51] Taubes was obliged to content himself with a reference to 1 Corinthians 7:29–31 as a provisional Pauline formulation of the mode of existence in the "now time."[52]

In this monograph, I restrict the group of philosophical interlocutors to those who have taken up the challenge of Taubes's insight into the implications of Paul's radical reduction of the dual commandment. Doubtless, I might have expanded and enriched my inquiry by engaging cultural critics such as Gayatri Spivak,[53] thereby alerting those who approach Paul out of a psychoanalytic-philosophical tradition to what may be missing from their conversations. The reader will eventually discover that my interpretation of Romans 13:8–14 lies closer to Julia Kristeva's reading of neighbor-love through Paul and Augustine: the strangeness of the neighbor is embraced within a new, singular universality through identification with the one who died for all.[54] Nevertheless, in order to maintain focus on the issues crucial to my interpretation of Romans 13:8–14 (the neighbor, the now time, an awakening of communal consciousness), I have restricted the circle of philosophical voices to those who have struggled with the consequences of Taubes's insight into the difficulty of Paul's ethical charge to love the other, following a trajectory that reaches from Benjamin to Santner.

I turn to analysis of the logic that connects these two paragraphs of Romans, first of all, as an historian and an exegete. That is to say, I will attempt to situate Paul's concept of the eschatological *kairos* and the "awakening" to which it summons in the context of first-century Judaism, seeking to discern whether Paul's thought is illuminated by apocalyptic parallels, such as *Psalms of Solomon* 17 and *Testament of Levi* 18,[55] or whether the Pauline *kairos* is more proximate to Jesus's proclamation of the nearness of the kingdom of God. I will attempt to deepen understanding of the presupposition of Paul's summons to "awakening" by exploring, selectively, the literature of the Silver Age, in which consciousness, both individual and collective, is depicted as sinking ever deeper into sleep.[56] I will contrast the dialectic of "awakening," as Paul understands it, with the frequent attempts by Hellenistic philosophers to rouse their contemporaries from moral lethargy.[57]

I will trace Paul's experience of the messianic *kairos* through his earlier epistles, in order to comprehend the particularity of that stage in the process of salvation which Paul images as "awakening" in Romans 13:11–14. Only then will I seek to clarify how Paul's eschatological faith enables his confidence in a community capable of obligating itself to mutual love.

2 | *KAIROS* (B)

ACCORDING TO PAUL, the possibility of executing the command to love the neighbor arises from an awareness, or recognition, of the *kairos* (Rom. 13:11). The opening of the paragraph that supplies the eschatological rationale for the love command has presented difficulties to interpreters, because the expression of Paul's thought is so compressed and pregnant: *kai touto eidotes ton kairon*, "And this knowing the *kairos*" (Rom. 13:11a).[1] Commentators endeavor to ameliorate the difficulty by supplying a finite verb, such as *poieite*: "And *you should do* this, knowing the *kairos*."[2] Others hypothesize that the expression *touto eidotes* is a citation formula introducing a baptismal or an Agape hymn, whose title was *ho kairos*, "The Critical Time," and whose stanzas are quoted in 13:11–12.[3] We should resist these speculative solutions and hold fast to the difficulty of the text as it stands, for this has the advantage of focusing our attention upon the integral relationship between knowledge and the *kairos*.[4] The extreme compression of Paul's rhetoric, which brings knowledge and the *kairos* into the closest proximity, suggests that the *kairos* is not a supramundane reality, which exists "out there," and arrives out of a divinely ordained future, but a temporal possibility that may be actualized in the moment when it is known, a moment that, as Paul goes on to explain, has the structure of "awakening."

But what is this *kairos* through whose straight gate one may enter into the capacity for neighbor-love? And how does Paul understand it? On this point, the commentators are virtually unanimous: to quote the most recent and most authoritative commentary, "The *kairos* mentioned here is the eschatological time that began with the sending of Christ and includes the expectation of the Messiah's return."[5] In support of this interpretation, reference is generally made to Jewish and Christian apocalyptic texts roughly contemporary with Romans.[6] Thus, in the *Psalms of Solomon*, which preserves the most detailed account of Jewish messianic expectation prior to Paul,[7] the "Lord Messiah" (17:32) "will gather a holy people whom he will lead in righteousness" (17:26); "He will judge peoples and nations in the wisdom of his righteousness" (17:29); "He will be compassionate to all the nations (who) reverently (stand) before him" (17:34); "Blessed are the ones born in those days" (17:44).[8] In the *Testament of Levi*, which, in its present form, is a Christian redaction of an older Jewish document,[9] the patriarch foretells the coming of a priestly Messiah: "Then the Lord will raise up a new priest to whom all the words of the Lord will be revealed. He will make a judgment of truth upon the earth for many days. And his star will rise in heaven like a king, kindling the light of knowledge as day is illumined by the sun. . . . He will take away all darkness from under heaven, and there shall be peace in all the earth" (18:2–4).[10] In the so-called Synoptic Apocalypse preserved in Mark 13,[11] the disciples are told: "Then they will see the Son of Man coming in the clouds with great power and glory. Then he will send out the angels, and gather his elect from the four winds, from the ends of the earth to the ends of heaven"

(Mark 13:26–27).[12] In all of these texts, the scheduled fulfillment of the divine plan is located in the future. In this context, Paul's mention of the *kairos* in Romans 13 is taken to be a reference to the return of Christ, in accordance with the expectation of the first generation of Christian converts.[13] If interpreters detect any nuance of difference between Romans 13 and the texts cited above, it is only that in Romans 13:11 they sense "a moving on of the eschatological clock,"[14] ticking more loudly as the time of Christ's *parousia* approaches.

But things are not so simple. There are clear indications that Paul is not referring to a future event, when he speaks of the *kairos* in Romans 13. As elsewhere in Romans when Paul mentions the messianic time (3:26; 8:18; 11:5), the term *kairos* is qualified by the temporal marker *nun*, which focuses attention on the present moment as such, "now."[15] In the third clause of Romans 13:11, the adverb *nun* is placed in emphatic position to make clear its connection to the aforementioned *kairos*.[16] Thus the "critical time" (*kairos*) of Romans 13:11 does not refer to a future Judgment Day in which Christians must prove themselves,[17] but designates the "time of the now," in cognizance of which one can fulfill the commandment to love the neighbor.[18] Moreover, the further temporal specification in the second clause of Romans 13:11, *hōra ēdē* (the hour [has come] already), suggests that the *kairos* intrudes into the present out of the past. The combination *hōra ēdē* is a colloquial expression found throughout ancient Greek,[19] including Matthew 14:15 (*hē hōra ēdē parēlthen*), meaning "it is now past time" or "the hour is now late."[20] The use of this expression indicates that the *kairos* has long since arrived. Finally, the point of reference for the comparative *egguteron* (nearer) in the last clause of Romans 13:11 locates "our salvation" in relationship to a past moment, "when we believed" (*hote episteusamen*).[21] In a manner that remains to be determined, Paul evidently conceives of the *kairos* as a relationship between the present moment and a definite previous one. Indeed, the presence of an antecedent moment within the *kairos* belongs to the logic of the image of "awakening" that Paul employs: something is already "there" to be grasped, in the flash of an awakened consciousness. Thus, those interpreters are wrong who contrast Romans 13:11–12 with other Pauline passages, such as 2 Corinthians 5:14–19, where it is clear that the Christ event has already occurred.[22] The *kairos* of Romans 13:11–12 does not refer to an event of the future, whether near or far.

It is the great virtue of the philosophical commentary on Romans by Giorgio Agamben to have decisively rejected the understanding of the Pauline *kairos* as an apocalyptic event.[23] Indeed, Agamben designates as "the most insidious misunderstanding" of the Pauline gospel that which mistakes *ho nun kairos* for the apocalyptic "end of time."[24] Agamben knows that, for Paul, "the Messiah has already arrived, the messianic event has already happened."[25] Yet, Agamben is unable to completely disenthrall himself from the spell of the future. Alluding to 1 Corinthians 7:29, Agamben insists that "what interests the apostle is not the last day, not the instant in which time ends, but the time that contracts itself and begins to end, the time that remains between time and its end."[26] Agamben visualizes the Pauline *nun kairos* as a brief span at the end of chronological time, a period that begins with Jesus's resurrection and lasts until the *parousia*.[27] Agamben is rightly concerned that the spatial character of his representation may result in a falsification of the Pauline *nun kairos*.[28] So Agamben has recourse to the concept of "operational time" proposed by the linguist Gustave Guillaume:[29] "According to Guillaume, the human mind experiences time, but does not possess the representation of it, and must, in representing it, take recourse to constructions of a spatial order."[30] The mental operation, however quick, in which an image of time is formed is what Guillaume calls "operational time."[31] Applying this concept to the Pauline *nun kairos*, Agamben proposes the following definition: "messianic time is the time we need to make time end: the time that is left us."[32] Thus, in the end, Agamben's conception of the structure of messianic time in Paul is rather traditional. Agamben writes: "Paul decomposes the messianic event into two times: resurrection and *parousia*, the second coming of Jesus at the end of time. Out of this issues the paradoxical tension between an *already* and a *not yet* that defines the Pauline conception of salvation."[33]

If one asks why the "now" of the Pauline *kairos* never arrives for Agamben, but is perpetually deferred, two answers present themselves—one superficial, the other more philosophical. First, Agamben circumscribes the *kairos* within chronological time. Although Agamben allows that "*ho nun kairos* does not coincide with secular chronological time, nevertheless," he insists, "it is *not outside* of chronological time either."[34] Agamben explains: "Messianic time is that part of secular time which undergoes an entirely transformative contraction."[35] What this involves, beyond images of foreshortening (such as "folding" or "furling"), is not clear.[36] But as a result of the presence of the messianic event within chronological time, the *parousia* is "stretched," in order "to make it graspable."[37] The *kairos* never arrives for Agamben, because it is bound to the march of the second hand, even if the hour lies so close to the Messiah's coming that it risks arriving before him.[38]

Second, and more importantly, Agamben's commitment to the philosophical project of knowledge as "the self-presence of consciousness" infinitely defers the *kairos* into a series of instants in which it is, or may be, "graspable."[39] Agamben's insistence that the "now" of the *kairos* is defined by the presence or proximity of a subject to itself guarantees that it can never be fully actualized; for, however great the speed of thought, it can "never coincide perfectly with itself, and the self-presence of consciousness consequently always takes on the form of time."[40] Thus, for Agamben, the *kairos* never arrests *chronos*, because self-consciousness constantly posits time.[41] Agamben's persistence in a philosophical perspective in which knowledge is reality contrasts with Paul's antiphilosophical proclamation of the *kairos* whose knowability as "awakening" cannot be reduced to positive knowledge.[42]

To summarize, Agamben's understanding of the Pauline *nun kairos* falls short of the apostle's conception in three respects. First, *kairos* and *chronos* are not genuinely opposed to each other in Agamben's philosophical interpretation; rather, "*kairos* is a contracted and abridged *chronos*."[43] In Agamben's lyrical image, "The pearl embedded in the ring of chance is only a small portion of *chronos*, a time remaining."[44] For Paul, by contrast, the *kairos* arrests and suspends *chronos*: its "now" is apart from the law of time (Rom. 3:21); it holds back the march of history toward judgment (Rom. 3:26); it is the birth canal of a new and glorious life (Rom. 8:18). Second, Agamben locates the *kairos* in a "here" and "now" defined by self-consciousness.[45] But the Pauline *kairos* cannot be reduced to self-consciousness; for Paul, only the Messiah brings the *kairos* that consummates history (Rom. 11:5–36). Finally, in Agamben, the *kairos* retains a future orientation: the presence of the *kairos* "stretches" time toward its *parousia*.[46] But for Paul, the *kairos* is a relationship between a past event and a potentiality in the present (Rom. 13:11–12). The consequence of these differences should not be underestimated. Because Agamben conceives of the *kairos* as "a time remaining" within *chronos*, he embraces the rabbinic apologue "for which the messianic world is not another world, but the secular world itself, with a slight adjustment."[47] This "slight difference" results from having grasped one's "disjointedness with regard to chronological time."[48] Agamben's "disjointedness" in time seems quite different from Paul's image of "awakening."

Since the philosophers seem to have failed us, I propose to seek an understanding of the Pauline concept of "the now time" by locating Paul's usage in relation to Jesus's proclamation of the "nearness" of the kingdom of God. I am led in this direction by remarkable and unexpected echoes of Jesus's message in Romans 13:11–12.[49] In Romans 13:12 Paul proclaims, *hē hēmera ēggiken* (the day is drawn near).[50] Commentators generally recognize that the closest parallel to Paul's statement is the saying of Jesus attested both in the Gospel of Mark (1:15) and in the Sayings Gospel Q (Luke 10:9, 10): *ēggiken hē basileia tou theou* (the kingdom of God is drawn near).[51] The difference, obviously, is that Jesus speaks of "the kingdom," whereas Paul refers to "the day." But in the Markan summary of Jesus's proclamation, the statement about the nearness of God's kingdom is the second hemistich of a synonymous parallelism, whose first line reads, *peplērōtai ho kairos* (the time is fulfilled), supplying another verbal overlap with Paul.[52] Most telling is the peculiar comparative *egguteron* (nearer) in Romans 13:11 describing the proximity of "our salvation": the term is *hapax legomenon* in the New Testament and, indeed, is unique in eschatological literature,[53] leaving no doubt that it is a Pauline echo of the language of Jesus.

What would it mean to locate the Pauline *kairos* in proximity to Jesus's proclamation of the nearness of the kingdom of God?

At first, the results for our understanding would appear to be negligible, since scholars of the historical Jesus are famously conflicted about the proper understanding of Jesus's eschatology.[54] At the beginning of the last century, Johannes Weiss and Albert Schweitzer represented the position of *apocalyptic eschatology*: Jesus thought that the kingdom would arrive in the immediate future; when it did not, he went to Jerusalem in order to compel the kingdom to come.[55] C. H. Dodd and his followers represent the position called *realized eschatology*: Jesus taught that the kingdom had already arrived, and was realizing itself in his words and deeds.[56] More recently, scholars such as John Dominic Crossan make a virtue of the seeming contradiction and seize upon the tension: the kingdom of God, they say, lives between the *already* and the *not yet*; it is the future will of God in the process of realization; the parables and aphorisms of Jesus are said to be characterized by a certain "tensiveness."[57]

But rather than resigning ourselves to this impasse, we should analyze more closely the summaries of Jesus's proclamation in Mark and Q, for in the reflected light of the Pauline appropriation, these summaries may disclose Jesus's understanding of the relationship between the kingdom of God and time. I suggest that it is not insignificant that the Markan summary of Jesus's proclamation takes the form of a synonymous parallelism, in which the second half-line of the verse says much the same thing as the first one, with variations.[58] Apart from the question whether this Hebraic form enhances the historical reliability of the saying,[59] the form directs our attention to the relationship that holds between the fullness of the *kairos* and the presence of God's reign. Translating the verb form *peplērōtai* so as to capture the full force of the perfect passive,[60] the Markan Jesus asserts that "the *kai-*

ros is filled full"; that is, there is no more place for *chronos*. Or, to use the language of time rather than space, *chronos* stands still and has come to a stop; the ceaseless progression of moments through homogeneous, empty time has been arrested. Time is "filled" with the presence of "the now." Further, the form of the synonymous parallelism implies that the fullness of time coincides with the advent of God's reign. In the thought of Jesus, as attested by both Mark and Q, the presence of God's reign manifests itself in the reversal of the intolerable constraints established by human sovereignty over the world: poverty, hunger, sadness, exclusion, violence (Luke 6:20–22).[61] Thus, the coming of God's kingdom is the end of human sovereignty.[62]

How are we to understand the synonymity of these statements—"the *kairos* is filled full" and "the kingdom of God is come near"? Here, I have recourse to the theory of enunciation developed by the linguist Émile Benveniste, not in order to clarify the thought of Jesus or Paul, but in order to expose our way of being in time as the root of our predicament. According to Benveniste, the capacity of human language to refer to itself, to its own taking-place, as a pure instance of discourse, goes hand in hand with "time-positing" (*chronothesis*), which is the origin of our representation of time; because Benveniste takes enunciation to be the foundation of subjectivity, the action of language in consciousness, as it seeks to coincide with itself, takes on the form of time.[63] To speak in a nonlinguistic fashion: subjectivity is constituted by the continuous projection of consciousness toward self-presence; this projection creates a continuum that we experience as time; within this continuum, the present is an empty transition. Our being in time takes the form of progression through a homogeneous continuum.[64]

Jesus's proclamation of the kingdom of God blasts open our temporal continuum. Jesus's announcement that "the *kairos* is filled full" aims at the arrest of our being in time, the standstill of our ceaseless projection of ourselves. The synonymous parallelism implies that only when a messianic cessation of time occurs does God begin to reign. The reign of God is the end of our time. It is our being shot through with the reality of God's reign. The paradox is that the end of our time is not the paralysis of our will, but the revolution of our will by the will of God.[65] That is to say, the proclamation of the reign of God calls for a decision, a radical change of heart, repentance (Mark 1:15), and a new social order. And because time is filled full, the choice must be made today. And the person who makes this choice chooses at a single stroke the whole of the future.

The similarity of the Jesus-tradition preserved in Mark 1:15 and QLuke 10:9–10 with Romans 13:11–12 suggests that Paul's concept of the *nun kairos* presupposes Jesus's proclamation of the kingdom of God.[66] Thus, for Paul, as for Jesus, the *kairos* is not an interval before the end of time, but time filled with the presence of the "now"; for Paul, as for Jesus, the *kairos* is not a transition to the future, but a present in which time stands still; for Paul, as for Jesus, the *kairos* cannot be deferred, but must be accepted today— "Behold, now is the acceptable time; behold, now is the day of salvation" (2 Cor. 6:2). Paul shares the understanding of the relationship between the kingdom of God and time attributed to Jesus in the tradition. But there is one crucial difference: whereas for Jesus the *kairos* is entirely present, for Paul the *kairos* is a relationship of the present to the past. According to Paul, the Messiah has already come, demonstrating "in the now time" God's righteousness toward the redemption of humanity through his death for the ungodly (Rom. 3:21, 26; 5:6–8), and inaugurating "in the now time" a new creation, glorious and reconciled (Rom. 8:18–25).[67] It is not clear that interpreters have yet taken sufficient account of the change in eschatology signified by Paul's conviction that the Messiah has already come.[68] In Romans 13:11–12, Paul attempts to convey the potentiality of the moment in which the past messianic event enters the present through the image of "awakening."

3 | AWAKENING (C)

WHAT IS THIS "awakening" (*egerthēnai*) that describes the process by which the past and present are concentrated in "the now time"? I propose to investigate the process that Paul images as "awakening" by excavating, first of all, the antecedent stage of consciousness that Paul's description invokes: namely, sleep (*hupnos*). While moral lethargy and even corruption and depravity are frequently represented as sleep in ancient literature,[1] there is a palpable density and gloominess about such images in the literature of the first century C.E.[2] In Seneca's *Hercules Furens*,[3] the characters move through "the desolation of everlasting night, and something worse than night."[4] "Sluggish Sleep" clings to the black, bedraggled foliage of the overhanging trees.[5] "The air hangs motionless, and black night broods over a torpid world."[6] Seneca pictures "the great throng which moves through the city streets, . . . some slow with age, gloomy and sated with long life; others of happier years, still able to run, maidens and youths,"[7] but all are "longing for sleep."[8] "All around is turbid emptiness, unlovely darkness, the sullen color of night, the lethargy of a silent world, and empty clouds."[9]

The "sleep" by which Seneca images the condition of his contemporaries is described as the "languid brother of hardhearted

Death,"[10] from whom fearful humans "gain knowledge of the long night" that is to come.[11] Death inhabits the rhythms of everyday life: dawn and birdsong awaken "hard toil, bestir every care"; crowds in the cities are "conscious of fleeting time," and seek to "hold fast the moments that will never return";[12] among the throngs moving through the streets, "each has a sorrowful sense of being buried beneath the earth."[13] A similar picture of life as a procession toward death appears in Seneca's *Oedipus*: "Each hour a new group files on toward Death, a long, sad column hastening in sequence to the shades; but the gloomy procession jams, and for the throng that seeks burial, the seven gates spread not wide enough. The grievous wrack of carnage halts, and funeral crowds funeral in unbroken line."[14] Seneca's comparisons of the crowds of the dead to the throngs of the living are instances of a phenomenon noted in several recent studies of Silver Age literature: the number of characters who seem to be dead before actually dying.[15] In this connection, we may observe that the infinitive *egerthēnai* that Paul employs in Romans 13:11 to describe the coming awakening ("to be roused, awakened") is used elsewhere in the New Testament in speaking of the resurrection of the dead.[16]

If we now wish to diagnose the causes, both proximate and ultimate, of this tendency in the literature of the early Empire to represent consciousness as sinking ever deeper into sleep, we do not have far to look, since Seneca provides glimpses of the underlying social and political realities, and since Paul himself names the dissipative behaviors by which the trance-like state was maintained among his contemporaries. When these literary allusions are correlated with the evidence that archaeology provides, a picture emerges of the violent and dehumanizing forces by which sovereign power was constituted and reconstituted in the early

Empire. From these forces, flight into unconsciousness was the natural response.

In Seneca's account of life in the cities, "overweening hopes stalk abroad, and trembling fears."[17] As examples, Seneca adduces the anxious client who "haunts the haughty vestibules and the unfeeling doors of his rich patrons,"[18] and the demagogue who is "dazed" by "popular acclaim" and "hoisted up by the mob, more shifting than sea-waves."[19] These and their like are "driven by the uncertainty of their fates to seek the Stygian waves of their own accord."[20] Seneca's gaze does not descend to the urban poor, whose living conditions had deteriorated sharply, owing to the rapid growth of Rome's population, the inconstancy of the food supply, the lack of proper sanitation and effective medicine, and the routine nature of violence.[21] Excavations outside the Esquiline Gate of Rome in the late nineteenth century revealed a mass grave that had been filled with twenty-four thousand corpses sometime in the late Republic, the dehumanizing end for thousands who had endured hard lives.[22] Nor does Seneca contemplate the fate of slaves, whose numbers had grown substantially, and who might be beaten and killed at their masters' discretion.[23] Along the road to Tibur, archeologists discovered a stone billboard advertising a torture and execution service operated by a group of funeral contractors who were open to business from private citizens and public authorities alike; there, slaves were flogged and crucified at a charge to their masters of four *sesterces* per person.[24]

Poverty and violence were proximate forces. The ultimate source of the "sleep" that descended over the early Empire was the new structure of power that emerged with Augustus and his successors.[25] The consolidation of power in the person of the emperor created degrees of dependent subjecthood, variously represented in the literature of the period as slavishness, unconsciousness, and living-death.[26] Seneca was all too aware of the transgressive pride that had plunged his world into a trance-like state. Seneca's Hercules wishes "to seize the highest realms . . . and snatch the scepter from his father";[27] he "seeks a path to heaven through ruin" and "desires to rule in an empty universe."[28] It is difficult not to see the bleak world depicted in Seneca's *Hercules* as anything other than a reflection of the macabre reign of Caligula,[29] who, according to Philo, "overstepped the bounds of human nature in his eagerness to be thought a god."[30] Caligula's megalomania and his unrestrained cruelty toward persons of all stations are vividly recounted by Suetonius.[31] To mention only one incident recorded by Cassius Dio, "once, when there was a shortage of condemned criminals to be given to the wild beasts, he [Caligula] ordered that a section of the crowd be seized and thrown to them instead; and to prevent the possibility of their making an outcry or uttering any reproaches, he first caused their tongues to be cut out."[32]

It would be a mistake to regard such incidents as manifestations of the personal depravity and insanity of a Caligula. The phenomenon was structural: terror was the means by which sole sovereignty was constituted and reconstituted in the Roman Empire.[33] In his *Res gestae*, Augustus boasts of having given gladiatorial games in which ten thousand men did battle to the death, and of having sent back thirty thousand runaway slaves to their masters for punishment;[34] Cassius Dio adds that those for whom no masters could be found were publicly impaled.[35] Suetonius's account of Claudius's cruelty is hardly less chilling than his report of Caligula: "At any gladiatorial show, either his own or another's, he [Claudius] gave orders that even those who fell accidentally should be slain, in particular the net-fighters [the *retiarii*, whose faces were not covered by helmets], so that he could watch their faces as they died."[36] Nor were such public dramatizations of the emperor's power restricted to Rome. In provincial cities such as Corinth, with its large amphitheater,[37] gladiatorial shows were closely associated with emperor worship.[38]

Consciousness sought refuge in spectacle entertainments.[39] The somnambulant throng moving through the city streets in Seneca's *Hercules* is "eager to see the spectacle in some new theater."[40] Tacitus complains: "There are special vices peculiar to this city which children seem to absorb, almost in the mother's womb: a partiality for the theater, and a passion for horse-racing, and gladiatorial shows."[41] In one of his letters to Lucilius, Seneca confronts the "compulsion" of his contemporaries "to watch the sufferings" of condemned criminals in the arena at Rome.[42] More than a hundred years after Seneca, Tertullian offered an explanation of the psychic lure of the gladiatorial shows: "They [the spectators] found comfort for death in murder."[43] But sometimes the mechanism failed to excite and distract. Seneca wrote to Lucilius that he went away from the staged execution of criminals feeling "more cruel and inhuman."[44] Ordinary spectators were sucked into the violence. Seneca reports the shouts of the spectators seated around him: "'Kill him!' they shout, 'Lash him! burn him!' 'Why does he meet the sword in so cowardly a way?' 'Why is he so frightened to kill?' 'Why so reluctant to die' 'Whip him to make him accept his wounds!'"[45] Sometimes the spectators turned the violence against one another, as one can see on the monument of Storax (figure 1), where a murderous brawl has broken out between ordinary people attending the munera,[46] and even more vividly on the large fresco that decorated the peristyle of a small house in Pompeii (figure 2), which depicts a full-scale riot that occurred in the amphitheater in 59 C.E.[47] Paradoxically, the spectacles to which people fled for amusement served to alienate human sociality from itself, reinforcing imperial sovereignty over all of life.

In Romans 13:13, Paul describes the dissipative behaviors by which sleep secured its hold over the multitude of his contemporaries: "revelries and drinking bouts, sexual excesses and debaucheries, quarreling and jealousy" (*kōmoi kai methai, koitai kai aselgeiai, eris kai zēlos*).[48] Noting the association of these activities with Roman dinner parties, recent interpreters take this verse as a warning against nocturnal behaviors that might trouble the Christian love-feast.[49] But in my view, a more relevant context is supplied by a painted frieze in the little Caupona of Salvius at Pompeii, which depicts four scenes of tavern life: two men being offered wine by a waitress, a woman and a man kissing, two men arguing over dice, and two men fighting.[50] Captions above the characters and clues encoded in the images themselves make it possible to infer the messages that these scenes would have communicated to the nonelite viewers for whom they were painted.[51] Two men, already intoxicated, compete for the wine that the barmaid carries, eagerly stretching out their hands (figure 3): the first man exclaims "Here!" (*hoc*), while his companion counters "No! It's mine!" (*non mia est*).[52] The image of the woman and the man kissing emphasizes the couple's eagerness for sexual contact, by the way in which their bodies are pressed together (figure 4); the man announces his licentious intent in the caption placed above his head: "I don't want to ... with Myrtalis" (*nolo cum Myrtale ...*), that is, he is done with Myrtalis and wishes to initiate a new sexual relationship with the woman he is kissing.[53] In the third scene, two men argue over gambling (figure 5): the man holding the dice-cup exclaims, "I won!" (*exsi*); the other insists, "It's not three; it's two" (*non tria duas est*). The disagreement turns violent on the final panel (figure 6), where the gamblers, now standing, come to blows. The men exchange insults: the first yells, "You nobody. It was three for me. I was the winner!" (*noxsi a me tria eco fui*); the other retorts, "Look here, cocksucker, I was the winner!" (*orte fellator eco fui*). The innkeeper intervenes: "Go outside and fight it out" (*itis foras rixsatis*).[54] The three behaviors (drunkenness, licentiousness, fighting) that Paul denotes by effective use of the trope of hendiadys[55] are vividly illustrated on the walls of the Caupona of Salvius; but while the tavern artist aimed to amuse,[56] Paul exposes, in melancholy earnest, "the works of darkness" (*ta erga tou skotous*) that must be "cast off," like entangling bed-coverings,[57] if his contemporaries are to awaken from sleep (Rom. 13:12).

To summarize, we return to Seneca's *Hercules Furens*, which has served so well as a cipher of sovereignty. After slaughtering his wife and children in an impious frenzy, Hercules falls asleep: "His eyelids fall in slumber, and his tired neck sinks beneath his drooping head; now his knees give way and his whole body goes crashing to the ground. . . . He sleeps; his chest heaves with measured breathing."[58] Amphitryon prays, "Let him have time for rest, that deep slumber may break the force of his madness and relieve his troubled heart."[59] And the chorus addresses a prayer to Sleep, with a voice that might have risen from the multitudes who endured the madness and crime of Caligula or Nero:[60] "And you, O Sleep, vanquisher of woes, rest of the soul, the better part of human life, . . . sluggish brother of cruel Death, . . . you who are peace after wanderings, haven of life, . . . who come alike to king and slave, hold him fast bound in heavy stupor; let slumber chain his unconquered limbs, and leave not his savage breast, until his former mind regains its course."[61] Yet, even as Hercules sleeps on the ground, "violent dreams are whirling in his fierce heart."[62] A "sleeping Hercules" is the emblem of the world that Paul and Seneca knew.

FIGURE 1
Detail of spectators fighting. Monument of Storax, pediment, left part

FIGURE 2
Riot in the amphitheater. House I, Pompeii, peristyle, northwest wall, 3, 23

FIGURE 3
Two male drinkers and a waitress. Caupona of Salvius, Pompeii

FIGURE 4
A woman and a man, kissing. Caupona of Salvius, Pompeii

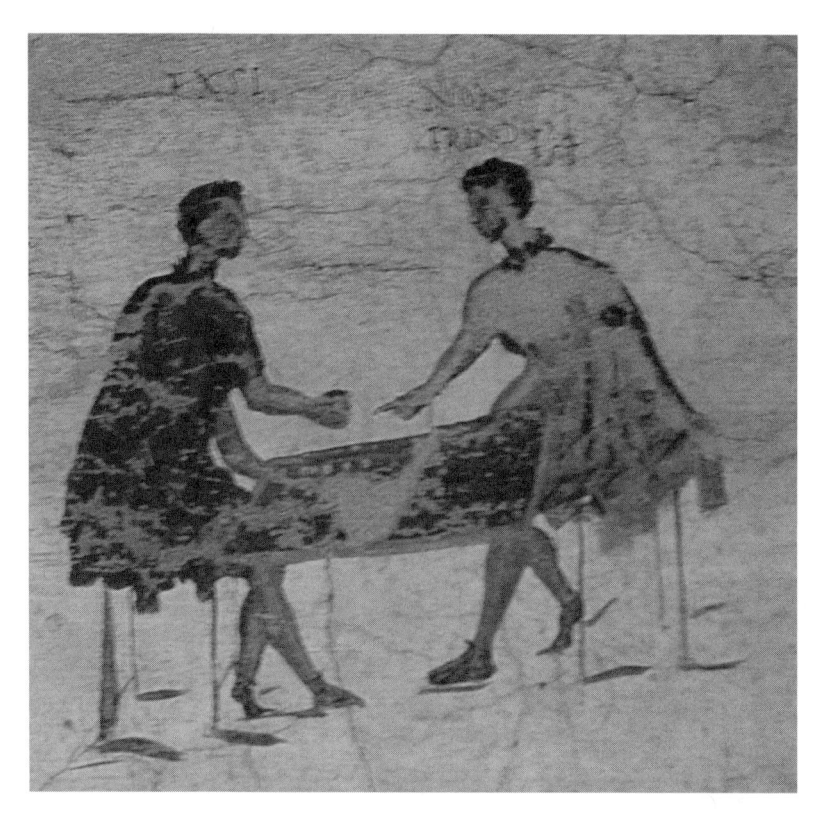

FIGURE 5
Two men arguing over dice. Caupona of Salvius, Pompeii

FIGURE 6
Two men fighting. Caupona of Salvius, Pompeii

4 | AWAKENING (C′)

THE MOMENT HAS now come to address the crucial question: what is the nature of the experience that Paul images as "awakening"? At first glance, it might seem that Paul's summons to awakening has much in common with the exhortations of Hellenistic philosophers to transcend base desires and overcome moral lethargy. Such admonitions occur frequently in the literature of this period, including the Jewish wisdom tradition.[1] In the pseudo-Platonic *Cleitophon*, Socrates's discourses to those who spend their energy on acquiring wealth, and who are mastered by their pleasures, are judged to be "truly capable of waking us up, as it were, out of slumber" (*atechnōs hōsper katheudontas epegeirein hēmas*).[2] In one of his diatribes, Epictetus argues that one such as Epicurus, who supposes the good to be nothing other than pleasure, says, in effect, to his followers: "Off to the couch and sleep, and lead the life of a worm, of which you have judged yourself worthy; eat and drink and copulate and defecate and snore."[3] The true philosopher, by contrast, is "aroused from his slumbers" (*egeiron auton ek tōn hupnōn*) by Nature herself, whose message he is to bequeath to others: "remain awake" (*agrupnēson*).[4] The sermon that concludes the *Poimandres* begins with the admonition: "O people, earth-born men, who have given yourselves over to drunkenness and sleep and ignorance of God, be sober, cease being intoxicated, entranced by irrational sleep" (*Ō laoi, andres gēgeneis, hoi methē kai hupnō heautous ekdedōkotes kai tē agnōsia tou theou, nēpsate, pausasthe de kraipalōntes, thelgomenoi hupnō alogō*).[5] As commentators have noted, the language of these philosophical admonitions is reminiscent of Romans 13:11–13.[6]

But just at the point of similarity, the difference stands forth with clarity: namely, in the *means* of "awakening." For the philosophers, the mechanism is knowledge of the self, self-mastery, or accommodation to the will of Nature. Cleitophon observes that Socrates's admonitions are based upon the premise that "a man should care above all for himself" (*pantōn heautou dei malista epimeleisthai*).[7] Cleitophon draws out the conclusion of Socrates's argument—"how that for every man who does not know how to make use of his soul, it is better to have his soul at rest and not to live" (*hōs hostis psuchē mē epistatai chrēsthai, toutō to agein hēsuchian tē psuchē kai me zen kreitton*).[8] Epictetus's answer to the question of what arouses a man from slumber is unequivocal: "What else but that which is the strongest thing in men—Nature, which draws a man to do her will, though he is reluctant and groans" (*ti gar allo ē to pantōn tōn en anthrōpois ischurotaton, hē phusis helkousa epi to hautēs boulēma akonta kai stenonta*).[9] Recalling that Orestes was "roused from his slumbers" (*ek tōn hupnōn exegeiresthai*) by the Furies, Epictetus exclaims: "Such a powerful and invincible thing is human nature!" (*houtōs ischuron ti kai anikēton estin hē phusis hē anthrōpinē*).[10] Thus, "self-control is good" (*agathon hē egkrateia*), in accordance with the sense given by Nature at birth.[11] The gnostic evangelist of *Poimandres* is awakened from sleep by "the mind of absolute mastery" (*ho tēs authentias nous*),[12] and instructed to "hold in your mind whatever things you wish to learn" *(eche nō sō hosa theleis mathein)*,[13] to "behold in mind the archetypal form" *(eides en tō nō to archetupon eidos)*.[14] In answer to the question "how shall I come to life again?" the gnostic is told: "The man who has mind in him, let him come to know himself" *(ho ennous anthrōpos anagnōrisatō heauton)*.[15] Summarizing his revelatory experience, the gnostic confesses: "For the sleep of the body became the soul's awakening" *(egeneto gap ho tou sōmatos hupnos tēs phuchēs nēpsis)*, and "All this befell me from my mind" *(touto de sunebē moi labonti apo tou noos mou)*.[16]

In respect to the means of awakening, the difference between Paul and his philosophical contemporaries could hardly be greater. Although the Pauline summons to awakening involves a kind of knowledge *(eidotes)*, the *object* of awareness is not the self, or nature, or mind, but the *kairos*—that is, the messianic event (Rom. 13:11). Indeed, as we shall see, the actualization of the relationship between knowledge and the *kairos* involves, for Paul, the death of the self, by means of a process that is antinatural, to some degree, and explicitly antiphilosophical.

According to Paul, "awakening" is an experience wherein the past event of the Messiah's death and resurrection comes together with the present moment in the life of believers, such that "salvation" acquires a higher degree of actuality than it had "when we [first] believed" (Rom. 13:11). Because Paul represents awakening as an increased concentration upon the messianic *kairos*—that is, upon an event that has already happened, and in which his Roman readers have already believed—we are justified in regarding awakening as a graduated process,[17] whose initial stages may be traced in Paul's earlier epistles.[18]

In Galatians 1:15–16, Paul looks back to the moment of his calling as an apostle of Messiah Jesus: "But when it pleased him [that is, God], the one who set me apart from my mother's womb and called me through his grace, to reveal his son in me, in order that I might preach him [that is, the Messiah] among the gentiles, immediately I did not confer with flesh and blood."[19] The crucial phrase, *apokalupsai ton huion auton en emoi*, has caused interpreters much consternation.[20] What kind of revelation does Paul have in mind? Evidently not a "vision" such as that attributed to Paul in the book of Acts.[21] When Paul speaks of visions elsewhere in his epistles, he uses forms of the verb *horan* (to see).[22] Paul's choice of the unusual term *apokaluptein* in Galatians 1:16 should be given full weight, and the verb should be translated literally: "to disclose," "to bring to light," "to unveil."[23] The preposition *en* in the phrase *en emoi* is not a substitute for the ordinary dative, denoting the object to which something happens, so that the phrase should be translated "to me."[24] Paul uses the same expression in Galatians 2:20 (*en emoi Christos*) where there is no possibility that the preposition denotes an object.[25] Thus, the entire phrase, *apokalupsai ton huion au tou en emoi*, suggests something latent in Paul that was "unveiled" by his first encounter with the messianic event.[26]

However elliptical Paul's account of his experience in Galatians 1:15–16 may be, there is no mystery about the content of the revelation: it was the death and resurrection of the Messiah.[27] It must be said that Paul places special emphasis upon the Messiah's *death* (2 Cor. 5:14; Rom. 5:6–8), even focusing upon the humiliating manner of his death—death on the cross (1 Cor. 1:18; 2:2; Phil. 2:8).[28] "The word of the cross is the power of God to us who are being saved," Paul declares (1 Cor. 1:18).[29] Paul insists that the Messiah died "for all" (2 Cor. 5:14–15), including the "weak" and the "ungodly" (Rom. 5:6), and especially, judging from the majority of those who responded to this message, the Messiah died for the "uneducated," the "powerless," the "low-born," that is, the "nothings and nobodies" (1 Cor. 1:26–28).[30]

At points, Paul provides glimpses of the effect of the messianic event upon himself and others. The inner experience disclosed in such passages is paradoxical in the extreme. In 2 Corinthians 5:14, Paul formulates the substance of the messianic event in the form of a premise: "One died for all" *(heis huper pantōn apethanen)*.[31] Paul represents this premise as something he has been able to "discern" *(krinantas touto)*, because "the love of the Messiah grasps us," or "holds us fast" *(hē agape tou Christou sunechei hēmas)*.[32] But the conclusion that one might expect from such a premise— "so that all might live," or "so that all might be spared death"—is not what follows; instead, Paul draws the emphatic inference: "so then all died" *(ara hoi pantes apethenon)*.[33] It is the same when Paul speaks in the first person in Galatians 2:19-20, whether the "I" *(egō)* is to be regarded as personal or paradigmatic: "I have been crucified with the Messiah; it is no longer I who live" *(Christō sunestaurōmai; zō de ouketi egō)*.[34] Finally, we may mention Romans 6:3-4, where Paul refers to the rite of initiation into the messianic community: "Do you not know that as many of us as have been baptized into Messiah Jesus were baptized into his death? *(ē agnoeite hoti, hosoi ebaptisthēmen eis Christon Iēsoun, eis ton thanaton autou ebaptisthēmen)*. Therefore we have shared a grave with him through baptism into death *(sunetaphēmen oun auto dia tou baptismatos eis ton thanaton)*."[35] We may add only that Paul's initial experience of the messianic event as a death of the self was not a one-time occurrence, but evidently accompanied him throughout his life as a servant of the Messiah. In 2 Corinthians 4:10-11, Paul reflects: "[We are] always carrying about in the body the death of Jesus *(hē nekrōsis tou Iēsou)*. . . . For while we live, we are always being handed over to death (*eis thanaton paradidometha*) on account of Jesus."[36]

This strange, unexpected consequence of the messianic event as Paul experienced it—namely, the death of the self—stands in striking contrast to the expectations voiced in nearly contemporary Jewish texts such as the *Psalms of Solomon*, where the Messiah confers upon those who belong to him wisdom, righteousness, and joy.[37] Of greater relevance to the present inquiry is the clean contradiction between Paul's account of his awakening and the ideal of self-recovery promoted by the philosophers sampled above. Indeed, Paul's approach seems to have more in common with that of the philosophical amateur Seneca, who saw death as the only way out of the nightmare of existence under Nero.[38] In his letters to Lucilius, Seneca returns repeatedly to the thought of suicide, directing his reader's attention to "any tree . . . any vein," as the path to freedom.[39] Seneca confesses to a longing for "death, little by little, in a steady weakening not without its pleasures, a peaceful annihilation I know well, having lost consciousness several times."[40] Eventually, as is well known, Seneca took this way out.[41] To return, one last time, to Seneca's *Hercules*, when the hero finally awakens from sleep in his right mind, and sees what he has done, his first thought is of suicide: "Why I should longer stay my soul in the light of day, and linger here, there is no cause. . . . By death must sin be healed."[42]

Yet the difference between Paul and Seneca with respect to the death of the self is obvious and significant.[43] For Paul, the messianic event has *partitioned* the self.[44] Only a part of Paul has died. To be sure, Paul speaks of this part as if it were the whole: "I no longer live" (Gal. 2:20a). But in each of the passages cited above, something lives on. In 2 Corinthians 5:15 Paul explains: "And he died for all, so that those who live might live no longer for themselves (*hina hoi zōntes mēketi heautois zōsin*), but for him who for their sake died and was raised."[45] So the part that dies is the self-seeking part; and the part that lives on has attached its being to the sacrificial death of the Messiah. Similarly, in Galatians 2:20 Paul declares: "I no longer live, but there lives in me Messiah (*zē de en emoi Christos*); and what I now live in the flesh, I live in the faith of the Son of God (*en pistei zō tē tou huiou tou theou*), who loved me and gave himself for me." So the part that dies is the part denoted by the first-person pronoun (*egō*), the egoistical part in its totality; and the part that lives on is the messianic seed, which was latent in Paul from the beginning (Gal. 1:15–16),[46] and has now been activated by the faithfulness of Messiah Jesus (cf. Gal. 2:16),[47] whose yes-saying to the love of God was so complete that he handed over his own life. One thing is clear: the messianic partition of the self that Paul experienced is not the body/soul dualism of the philosophers, on the basis of which the philosophers practice "the art of dying."[48] The Messiah who now lives in Paul "lives in the *flesh*" (Gal. 2:20); the "life of Jesus" that is "manifested" on the other side of death is "manifested in our *bodies* . . . manifested in our *mortal flesh*" (2 Cor. 4:10–11).[49] The messianic partition of the self divides the totality of Paul's being. Paul has passed through death, held fast by the intensity of the Messiah's love, "participating in his sufferings, becoming like him in his death" (Phil. 3:10). Only the messianic remnant remains, lives on in hope of resurrection (Phil. 3:11; Rom. 6:4).

5 | *KAIROS* (B′)

WE MAY NOW seek to comprehend the particularity of that stage in the process of salvation that Paul images as "awakening" in Romans 13:11–14. In what way does this experience differ from the antecedent stages in the process—calling, revelation, death-and-resurrection of the self, bearing about of the Messiah's dying-and-rising through the world? We may begin with clues in the text of Romans 13:11–14.[1]

First, awakening is characterized by proximity—a proximity that is both spatial and temporal: "our salvation is *nearer* (*egguteron*) than when we first believed" (Rom.13:11); "the day is drawn near (*ēggiken*)."[2] Perhaps we can circumscribe this spatial and temporal proximity in the concept of *actuality*: in awakening, everything that belonged to the messianic *kairos* acquires a higher degree of actuality than it had in the previous instances of its existence.

Second, there is an unmistakable *militancy* about the imagery with which Paul describes the awakened consciousness to which he summons his readers: "Let us therefore cast off the works of darkness, and let us put on the armor of light (*endusōmetha de ta hopla tou photos*)" (Rom. 13:12b).[3] The association of light with weapons and warfare is found in Jewish apocalyptic literature.[4]

Anticipating the final battle between the "sons of light" and the "sons of darkness," the War Scroll from Qumran praises God: "You have appointed the day of battle from ancient times . . . to come to the aid of truth and to destroy iniquity, to bring darkness low and to magnify light . . . to stand forever, and to destroy all the sons of darkness."[5] Employing similar imagery, Paul pictures the moment of awakening as a readiness for battle, conveying the inner transformation required by using the middle voice of the verb *enduō*—"gird oneself."[6]

Third, it is noteworthy that all of the personal pronouns in Romans 13:11–14, whether first or second person, are plural. The pronominal subject of the infinitive *egerthēnai* in Romans 13:11b may have been *humas* (you), or the somewhat less well-attested *hēmas* (us);[7] but, in any case, it is a *collective subject*, and not merely an individual consciousness, which is summoned to awakening. Similarly, in Romans 13:11c, Paul speaks of "*our* salvation" (*hēmōn hē sōtēria*), with the pronoun in the emphatic position. The verbal forms of address are also plural, whether hortatory or imperatival: *apobalōmetha*, "let us cast off" (Rom. 13:12c); *endusōmetha*, "let us put on" (Rom. 13:12d); *peripatēsōmen*, "let us conduct ourselves" (Rom. 13:13); *endusasthe*, "gird yourselves" (Rom. 13:14a); *mē poieisthe*, "do not make" (Rom. 13:14b). In these exhortations, commentators sense Paul's attempt to engender solidarity among members of the congregation.[8] Obviously, awakening was a process in the life of the individual. But the *collective* character of the experience is emphasized in this paragraph.

Fourth, Paul focuses upon concrete behaviors that must be put aside, if awakening is to occur: drunkenness, debauchery, quarreling (Rom. 13:13b). Correspondingly, he emphasizes the decency of conduct (*euschēmonōs peripatēsōmen*) that must characterize the awakened life (Rom. 13:13a).[9] To be sure, ethical admonitions to a transformed life are found in most Pauline epistles. Distinctive here is the intensity of interest, the urgency to commence (signaled by the ingressive aorist subjunctive of *peripateō*),[10] and the intimacy of connection (conveyed by the mystical exhortation to "put on [*endusasthe*] the Lord Jesus Messiah" [Rom. 13:14a], like a tunic).[11] There is, one might say, an interpenetration of the self with specific modes of conduct in 13:11–14 that gives to waking-being a *higher concretion*.

Finally, the summons to awakening as a whole suggests that the moment is *probative* in a final sense. "The day" (*hē hēmera*) that has "drawn near" (*ēggiken*) is a judgment day, in which each of the antecedent stages of "salvation" will be put to the test. Will the process that began "when we first believed" (Rom.13:11c) achieve critical mass, so to speak, so that it combusts? The choice on that day is absolute: "Clothe yourselves in the Lord Jesus Messiah, and make no provision (*pronoian mē poieisthe*) for the flesh, toward desires" (Rom. 13:14). The expression *pronoian poieisthai* (to make provision) is an idiom of business life.[12] The test is this: will it be possible, on the day of awakening, to suspend the routine mechanism of self-interest, the constant projection of thought toward desire, so that existence is completely enveloped in the Messiah?

Whatever insight these observations may provide into the experience of awakening described in Romans 13:11–14, they do not yet penetrate to the core of Paul's conception, which is irreducibly eschatological. The awakening to which Paul summons results, in the last instance, from a "knowing" or "discerning" (*eidotes*) of the *kairos* (Rom. 13:11a). In awakening, the decisive event of the past (the Messiah's advent) is brought together with the present (the now of salvation) as a potential for knowledge. But why does Paul choose the image of a suddenly emergent consciousness to convey the eschatological constellation between past and present? Or, to put it another way: how does the image of awakening in Romans 13 express Paul's mature conception of the relation of past and present in "the now time"?

Perhaps the best prospect of finding an answer to this question lies in a comparison of the eschatology of Romans 13:11–14 with that of Paul's earliest extant letter, 1 Thessalonians.[13] In response to the concerns of the Thessalonian believers about "times and seasons" (1 Thess. 5:1), Paul reminded them of his teaching about the "day of the Lord" (1 Thess. 5:2–10):

> The day of the Lord (*hēmera kuriou*) comes like a thief in the night. When they say "peace and security" (*eirēnē kai asphaleia*), then sudden destruction comes upon them, like birth-pains come upon a pregnant woman, and they shall in no way escape. But you, brothers, are not in darkness (*ouk este en skotei*), so that the day should catch you like a thief; for you are all sons of light and sons of day (*pantes gap humeis huioi photos este kai huioi hēmeras*). We are not of night or of darkness (*ouk esmen nuktos oude skotous*). So then let us not sleep like the others (*ara oun mē katheudōmen hōs hoi loipoi*), but let us be alert and sober (*alla grēgorōmen kai nēphōmen*). For those sleeping sleep at night (*hoi gar katheudontes nuktos katheudousin*), and those getting drunk get drunk at night (*kai hoi methuskomenoi nuktos methuousin*). But since we are of the day (*hēmeis de hemeras ontes*), let us be sober, putting on (*endusamenoi*) the breastplate of faith and love, and as a helmet the hope of salvation, because God did not destine us for wrath, but to obtain salvation (*sōtēria*)

through our Lord Jesus Messiah, the one who died for us, so that whether we are awake or asleep *(eite grēgorōmen eite katheudōmen)*, we might live with him.

It is immediately apparent how much this passage has in common with Romans 13:11–14, not only in terms of imagery, but also in vocabulary.[14] In both cases, Paul speaks of "day" *(hēmera)* and "night" *(nux)*, of "light" *(phōs)* and "darkness" *(skotos)*. Both passages mention "drunkenness" *(methuō/methē)* as a paradigmatic vice. Both texts employ the verb *enduō* in exhortations to "put on" spiritual armor. In both cases, the divinely destined goal is "salvation" *(sōtēria)*. In both places, Paul employs the formula "Lord Jesus Messiah" *(kurios Iēsous Christos)*.

At the center of both passages stands the contrast between sleep and waking; but in this case, the vocabulary is different, and the difference is significant. In 1 Thessalonians 5:2–10, Paul uses the verbs *katheudō* and *grēgoreō* to speak of being asleep and remaining awake, and does not employ the vocabulary of Romans 13:11, neither the noun *hupnos* nor the verb *egeirō*.[15] In Romans 13:11, by contrast, Paul does not recur to the terms *katheudō* or *grēgoreō*.[16] The difference is not merely terminological, but conceptual. The action denoted by *katheudō* is "lying down to sleep," "lying idle," "passing the night in sleep."[17] But *hupnos* is the state of "sleep," in which one dreams, from which one wakes.[18] As a powerful and all-encompassing state,[19] *hypnos* was hypostasized as a god—the son of Night,[20] the twin-brother of Death.[21] The condition described by *grēgoreō* is "being watchful" or "remaining alert";[22] thus the noun *grēgorēsis* is "wakefulness."[23] By contrast, *egeirō* marks the moment of arousal, the transition out of sleep: thus, to "wake up," to "awaken."[24]

The crucial difference between 1 Thessalonians 5 and Romans 13 with respect to the imagery of sleeping and waking is a difference between the static and the dynamic. In 1 Thessalonians 5, Paul contrasts two conditions: on the one hand, those who are asleep in their own lives, intoxicated—the sons of night and darkness;[25] on the other hand, those who are alert and sober—the sons of light and day.[26] In abstract terms, the contrast is between consciousness and unconsciousness. But in Romans 13, Paul focuses upon the moment of transition, the instant of awakening.[27] Awakening relates to sleep in Romans 13:11 precisely in being separated from it (*ex hupnou egerthēnai*); that is, the structure of awakening is dialectical. Thus, awakening in Romans 13 is a distinctive experience, to be distinguished both from consciousness and from unconsciousness.

Another, more precise difference between 1 Thessalonians 5 and Romans 13 appears in the way in which night and day are contrasted. In 1 Thessalonians 5:5–8, the contrast is static and absolute: night and day are discrete periods, each with its own denizens (1 Thess. 5:5), each spawning its own behaviors (1 Thess. 5:7–8).[28] But Romans 13:12 focuses upon the moment of turning from night to day.[29] The punctual nature of the contrast is emphasized by Paul's use of a vivid expression for the night approaching its end: *hē nux proekopsen* (the night is far gone).[30] The aorist of the verb *prokoptō* suggests "the time of night when especially deep darkness holds sway just before dawn."[31] Again, the image is dialectical: day relates to night precisely at the moment of separation.

I suggest that the different ways in which sleeping and waking, night and day, are imaged in 1 Thessalonians 5 and Romans 13 reflect a significant development in Paul's eschatology.[32] The eschatology of 1 Thessalonians may be characterized as primitive. Paul's consolation of the bereaved in 1 Thessalonians 4:13–18 cites an apocalyptic "word of the Lord" (1 Thess. 4:15–16).[33] The saying about the day of the Lord that comes like a thief in the night in 1 Thessalonians 5:2 is based upon traditional material (cf. Rev. 3:3).[34] The slogan "peace and security" (*eirēnē kai asphaleia*) cited in 1 Thessalonians 5:3 has its closest parallel in Jewish literature in the messianic *Psalms of Solomon* (8:18).[35] The orientation of 1 Thessalonians is entirely toward the future. Paul reminds the Thessalonians of how they responded to his preaching: they determined "to wait for the Son out of the heavens, whom he [that is, God] raised out of the dead, Jesus the one who saves us from the coming wrath" (1 Thess. 1:10).[36] Paul's consolation to the bereaved is that "God will bring those who have died in the Messiah with him" when he returns (1 Thess. 4:13–18).[37] Only twice in 1 Thessalonians (4:14; 5:10) does Paul speak of the death of Jesus, and that only in passing. By contrast, all of the references to the second "coming" (*parousia*) of Messiah Jesus in the authentic Pauline epistles, with one exception (1 Corinthians 15:23), are found in 1 Thessalonians (2:19; 3:13; 4:15; 5:23).[38]

A striking contrast is presented by Romans with respect to Paul's eschatology. As noted, the term *parousia* is missing.[39] And, indeed, there are no unambiguous references to the Second Coming of Jesus.[40] To be sure, Paul still speaks of "a day of wrath and revelation of the righteous judgment of God" (Rom. 2:5),[41] and looks forward to "the coming glory to be revealed" when "the creation itself will be set free from its bondage to decay" (Rom. 8:18, 21).[42] But it is clear that, for the author of Romans, the messianic event has already occurred. That event is the death and resurrection of the Messiah (Rom. 8:34).[43] "The righteousness of God has been manifested ... through the faith of Jesus Messiah" (Rom. 3:21–22).

"At the *kairos*, the Messiah died for the ungodly" (Rom. 5:6).[44] "God demonstrates his love for us in that while we were still sinners the Messiah died for us" (Rom. 5:8). This "righteous act" of Messiah Jesus has inaugurated a new creation (Rom. 5:18–19; cf. 2 Cor. 5:17). Henceforth, "nothing will be able to separate us from the love of God in Messiah Jesus our Lord" (Rom. 8:39).

In seeking to understand this development in Paul's eschatology, we must bear in mind the number of years that have passed between 1 Thessalonians and Romans: 1 Thessalonians is Paul's earliest extant letter, and as such the oldest writing in the New Testament.[45] According to a broad critical consensus, Romans is the last authentic Pauline epistle.[46] Depending upon which chronology of Paul's life and letters one adopts, as few as six or as many as fourteen years separate Paul's first and last letters.[47] In any case, Paul had suffered and learned much in the intervening years: he had been imprisoned and tortured on account of Messiah Jesus (2 Cor. 11:23–25; Phil. 1:7, 13).[48] Not surprisingly, he contemplated his own death, anticipating that his life might be "poured out as a libation upon a sacrificial altar" (Phil. 2:17), imagining what it would be like to be "away from the body and at home with the Lord" (2 Cor. 5:8; cf. Phil. 1:23).[49] In moments of crisis, it seems that Paul appropriated the event of the crucified Messiah more deeply as the truth of his own life (2 Cor. 4:7–12; 12:9–10).[50] In my view, it would be a mistake to attempt to explain the development in Paul's eschatology as a rationalizing response to the specious problem of the "delay of the *parousia*."[51] Indeed, I would argue that the mature eschatology of Romans reflects an *intensification* of expectation:[52] "Our salvation is nearer than when we first believed," Paul declares (Rom. 13:11). By the time Paul wrote Romans, the future hope of Paul's early years had become a present reality,[53] to be grasped in a moment of awakening.

We may now summarize what we have learned about the awakening to which Paul summons in Romans 13 as the culmination of Pauline eschatology. Paul urges his readers toward a moment when the full import of the messianic event will be received in the present as an actuality. In that moment, the latent messianic self that was unveiled in the calling, and that had emerged through participation in the Messiah's death and resurrection, ignites in the flash of an awakened consciousness. In that moment, the constant projection of thought toward desire is arrested; the existence of the believer is enveloped in the Messiah. The awakened self takes charge of his conduct, giving each action a higher ethical purpose. The awakened self is a militant, armed for struggle against the powers of darkness that had once enthralled him and that still hypnotize others. And the awakened self participates in a collective consciousness, bound to others by the love that led the Messiah to die for all. The community of awakened selves is "the revelation of the sons of God" (*hē apokalupsis tōn huiōn tou theou*) for which the whole creation waits with eager longing (Rom. 8:19).[54]

6 | NEIGHBOR (A′)

How does an awakening among those who have discerned the *kairos* make it possible to fulfill the command to love the neighbor? Or how does the eschatological faith professed in Romans 13:11–14 empower the political ethics enjoined in Romans 13:8–10? Or, once again, how does the messianic temporality of awakened-being liberate persons so that they may obligate themselves to mutual love?

Again, we start from features of the text. First, the capacity to obligate oneself to mutual love arises only when all other obligations have been renounced: "Owe no one anything (*mēdeni mēden opheilete*), except to love one another" (13:8a). The verb *opheilō* denotes financial, legal, or social obligation—so, indebtedness.[1] But it would be a mistake to interpret Paul's admonition as an extension of conventional advice against incurring debts.[2] Paul's injunction is sweeping: "owe nothing to anyone"—the force of the injunction intensified by the use of the present imperative form of the verb.[3] The structure of obligation in the Roman world was patronage, "an asymmetrical personal relationship involving reciprocal exchange."[4] In practice, patronage was a means of social control through the manipulation of access to scare resources.[5] The system of obligation even extended to slaves, through the institution of *peculium*, "property, in whatever form, assigned for use, within limits, to someone who lacked the right of property, either a slave or someone in *patria potestas*."[6] Roman society was organized as a pyramid of obligation, with the emperor as supreme patron.[7] Paul's admonition to unplug from the patronage system may seem a hopelessly utopian gesture, an impression reinforced by the fact that the closest parallels to Paul's expression *mēdeni mēden opheilete* are found in comedy and on tombstones—the wish of a poor man, the praise of a virtuous wife.[8] And yet, it is clear that Paul intends for his admonition to be taken seriously. Paul himself refused a gift, and thereby declined an offer of patronage from a wealthy believer at Corinth (1 Cor. 9; 2 Cor 11:7–11).[9] How radical would Paul's admonition have seemed to his Roman readers? Even if some of the Roman assemblies met in tenements (*insulae*), rather than houses (*domus*) with patrons,[10] they would not have been free of the obligations imposed by various forms of economic, legal, and social dependency in their daily lives.

Second, the alternative to patronage is represented as a form of mutualism: "Owe no one anything, except to love one another (*ei mē to allēlous agapan*)." The particles *ei mē* designate an inclusive exception: a new and singular obligation is to replace social and economic dependency upon patrons.[11] The articular infinitive *to agapan* is totalizing: not discrete acts, but a whole way of life is enjoined upon believers, the anaphoric reference of the article indicating that the command was already well known.[12] Several scholars have recently and rightly argued that Paul advocated the practice of economic mutualism as a survival strategy among members of his messianic assemblies.[13] Moreover, the collection for "the poor among the saints in Jerusalem" (Rom. 15:26), upon which Paul labored for many years, is best understood as an ecumenical extension of mutualism as an alternative to patronage.[14] The challenge for Paul, as the agent of mutualism, was that the group designated by the reciprocal pronoun *allēlous* (one another) in Romans 13:8a was a diverse group, including slaves and free, Jews and gentiles, women and men, poor and rich.[15] The practice of mutualism among the members of such a group would have entailed significant voluntary redistribution of resources.[16] At least this was the case at Corinth, where a few wealthy believers, such as Crispus and Gaius (1 Cor. 1:14; Rom. 16:23),[17] had joined a congregation whose majority consisted of the poor, the uneducated, and the lowborn (1 Cor. 1:26–28; 11:21–22).[18] This was also the case in the partnership between the Corinthians, whose "abundance" Paul emphasizes, and the saints in Jerusalem, who suffered "lack" (2 Cor. 8:14).[19] In advocating mutualism, Paul revived the old Greek ideal of "equality" (*isotēs*), and gave it a new theological basis in the self-impoverishment of Messiah Jesus (2 Cor. 8:9–15).[20] Paul's promotion of mutualism, like his injunction against patronage, seems wildly utopian. But, again, it is clear that Paul intended his admonition to be taken literally and applied practically. This is indicated, among other things, by Paul's recurrence to the language of obligation in the rationale that he provides for the contribution of the Macedonians and Achaeans to the poor in Jerusalem in Romans 15:27: "Indeed, they owed it to them (*kai opheiletai eisin autōn*); for if the gentiles have partaken in their spiritual goods, they are obligated to render them services also in material things (*opheilousin kai en tois sarkikois leitourgēsai*)."[21] Once again, we may ask how radical Paul's advocacy of mutualism would have seemed to his Roman readers. Most of the Christian assemblies at Rome comprised slaves and the poor, as their location in the harbor district of Trastevere and in the damp and heavily trafficked valley of the Porta Capena suggests.[22] But more affluent Christians may have assembled in other districts, such as Mars field and the Aventine, regions that show evidence of a Christian population at a later period.[23]

Third, the object of love is described as the embodiment of difference: "for the one who loves *the other (ho gar agapōn ton heteron)* has fulfilled the law" (13:8b).[24] Paul's choice of the term *heteros* (other) to designate the object of love is surprising.[25] The expected object of the verb *agapaō* is either "brother" or "neighbor," given the citation of Leviticus 19 to which Paul's formulation looks forward.[26] In Leviticus 19:17–18, the neighbor is "your kinsperson," one of "the sons of your people."[27] But in the term *heteros* a clear nuance of difference resides.[28] Embraced within this difference are differences in ethnicity, status, and gender that characterized the membership of Paul's messianic assemblies (Gal. 3:28; cf. 1 Cor. 12:13).[29] The obligation of mutual love not only traverses these distinctions,[30] but embraces "the other" as the embodiment of difference. Paul's choice of the word "other," rather than "neighbor" or "brother," was no doubt intended to short-circuit the widespread assumption in Greco-Roman society that true love depended upon sameness, affinity, and familiarity, and that the true friend was a "mirror of the self."[31] The sweeping nature of Paul's formulation suggests that Paul had in mind not just particular cases, but the ethic of the community: a community that practices love of "the other" can never be a totality—that is, a group closed upon itself. A people that practices love of "the other" is perpetually incomplete.[32]

Fourth, Paul asserts that love of the other accomplishes the law's original purpose: "for the one who loves the other has fulfilled the law *(nomon peplēro͞men)*". The *nomos* under consideration here is the best and highest law known to Paul, the Mosaic Torah, as demonstrated by the four commandments from Deuteronomy 5:17–21 and Exodus 20:13–17 (LXX) cited in 13:9.[33] The fact that the word *nomos* is used here without the article may suggest that Paul also wishes his readers to think of "law" in a generic sense.[34] In any case, the echo of the Jesus tradition in the verb *plē̄roō̄* is crucial: as in Matthew 5:17, to "fulfill" the law is to penetrate to its root.[35] And, Paul asserts, we come closest to the original intent of the law in the one "word" that "summarizes" or "recapitulates" all the commandments: "You shall love your neighbor as yourself" (13:9).[36]

These observations prepare us to address the final question: how does an awakening among those who have grasped the full import of the Messiah's death and resurrection make possible the execution of the command to love the neighbor? The signpost to the right path is found in the command itself: "You shall love your neighbor as yourself" (*agapēseis ton plēsion sou hōs seauton*). All love is directed toward an object, even if that object is the self.[37] But the kind of love varies with the object: libidinal love seeks the object of desire; spiritual love is evoked (or enforced) by the divine, even if God is conceived psychologically as the superego or the apex of the symbolic order.[38] The third love, love of neighbor, is the most difficult of the three, because it requires the highest degree of resolve. Rabbinic commentators on Leviticus 19:18 were already familiar with this distinction and saw it embodied in a peculiarity of the biblical text, where the Hebrew verb *'ahab*, "love," takes the preposition *le*, rendered "to, for, on behalf of, for the sake of."[39] Love of a woman or love of God, by contrast, is denoted by *ahab* plus the object marker (*nota accusativi*) *'t*.[40] The immediacy of attraction that a man feels for a woman whom he sees on the other side of the road or the rapture with which a person finds that he or she has been singing *kadosh* (holy, holy, holy!) in a morning dream just before waking are not operative in the case of the neighbor. There is a gap that requires resolve, a motion of the will, a conscious choice—a gap denoted and covered by the preposition *le*.

Although thinking and writing in Greek rather than Hebrew, Paul was familiar with the different kinds of love and the greater sacrifice required in order to love the neighbor. In a foundational text, Paul explains: "For while we were still weak, the Messiah died at the *kairos* on behalf of the ungodly. Scarcely on behalf of a righteous person will someone die, though perhaps on behalf of a good person someone might dare to die. But God demonstrates his own love (*agapē*) toward us, in that while we were still sinners the Messiah died for us" (Rom. 5:6–8).[41] Paul can imagine, with difficulty, cases where a righteous person or a good person might evoke love sufficient for a self-sacrificial act. But Paul is unable to speak of death for the weak, ungodly, and sinners without reference to the love of God. Taking this passage as the messianic foundation of the ethic enjoined in Romans 13, we may now draw an inference: one who has awakened to the messianic nature of his or her own existence is empowered to do the most difficult thing—the thing that Freud, as Paul's spiritual heir, rightly judged to be unreasonable and impossible in human terms: to love the neighbor. But we should bear in mind that, according to Paul, there is no unmediated access to the strength to love the neighbor. The passage to such an extraordinary love leads through messianic suffering (Rom. 5:3–5).[42]

If the commandment, in the context of Paul's messianic faith, furnishes an index to the means of its fulfillment, we have nevertheless discovered that the *subject* of the awakening is not the individual in isolation, however intense and genuine his experience may be, but the community of those who have been "called," the *ekklēsia*. Just as in Romans 13:11–14, where the personal pronouns and the verbs of address are plural, so in 13:8 the imperative (*opheilete*) is plural and the pronoun (*allēlous*) is a reciprocal plural. How, then, does a *collective subject*, awakened to its messianic life, put into practice the ethic of neighbor-love?

As a heuristic, we may compare Paul's idea of awakened communal consciousness with another vision of collective subjectivity that has inspired political action in the modern period—the Marxist idea of class consciousness. Here we must proceed cautiously, with due attention to historical circumstances, so that our comparison should not be superficial, but differential. Once again, we have Giorgio Agamben as predecessor, since he contemplates the comparability of the Pauline and the Marxian concepts of "class" in his discussion of the messianic vocation (*klēsis*) in Romans.[43] However, for us, the point of comparison is not the concept of class, but of class consciousness.

We take it as established that classes existed in Paul's world, insofar as "class" is defined as an economic relation that separated one's mode of life, interests, and culture from those of other groups and placed them in opposition to one another.[44] But it is a legitimate question whether, and how far, class consciousness existed among the subelite in antiquity.[45] Of this there are only sporadic glimmerings: for example, the social revolution in the Achaean town of Dyme in 116–114 B.C.E.,[46] the slave revolt led by Spartacus in 73–71 B.C.E.,[47] the protest of the *plebs* of Rome against the mass execution of the slaves of Pedanius Secundus in 61 C.E.;[48] perhaps we should also include the "conspiracy" at Cibyra (on the border of Phrygia and Caria) in 23 C.E., in connection with which

107 public slaves escaped from their condition.[49] These tremors of "awakening" were vigorously suppressed by the authorities: two of the leaders of the revolt at Dyme were immediately condemned to death by the proconsul, while another was sent to Rome for trial;[50] six thousand captured followers of Spartacus were crucified along the Appian Way from Capua to Rome;[51] Nero suppressed the riot of the *plebs* against the execution of four hundred slaves of Pedanius Secundus by lining the whole length of the road along which the condemned were marched to their deaths with detachments of soldiers.[52]

The sources, produced almost entirely by the elite, are no doubt partly to blame for the paucity of evidence of class consciousness among the poor in antiquity. For example, our only evidence for the events in Dyme is an inscription recording a letter of the proconsul Q. Fabius Maximus to the city of Dyme, which complains bitterly of the cancelation of debts and of the enactment of legislation "contrary to the constitutions granted to the Achaeans by the Romans"[53]—a reference to the oligarchical governments imposed upon the cities of the Peloponnese by Lucius Mummius, after crushing the revolt of the Achaean League in 146 B.C.E.[54]

Whatever limitations are imposed by the sources, it is clear that the constitution of sovereign power in Rome depended upon the maintenance of a system of distinctions between classes that was both symbolic and frighteningly real.[55] Citizens were distinguished from noncitizens, free from slaves. Certain persons were categorized as *infames*—actors, prostitutes, gladiators; thus, they did not enjoy inviolability of the body, and might be beaten or killed with impunity.[56] Seneca reports the diverse means of torture that he had seen masters use against their slaves: "some hang their victims with head toward the ground, some impale their private parts, others stretch out their arms on a fork-shaped gibbet."[57] In those places where the populace came together, the theater and the amphitheater, the segregation of seating reinforced stratification.[58] The Augustan Lex Julia Theatralis,[59] a law renewed by Claudius and Nero,[60] rigidly segregated spectators into different social groups, each with a preassigned seating area, accessible via a specific entryway,[61] a hierarchical arrangement also adopted in civic arenas in Roman colonies.[62] The entertainment offered in the amphitheater—beast fights, executions of criminals, gladiatorial combats—ritually reconstituted the order of power.[63] In all these ways, Roman authorities suppressed the development of an ideology that might bind elements of the populace together and sustain a program of action.[64]

As is well known, the Marxist theorist of class consciousness, according to Georg Lukács, argued that class consciousness was unable to achieve complete clarity in antiquity because the various sectors of society remained unaware of the economic basis of the problems and conflicts with which they were afflicted.[65] Instead, individuals and groups assumed that their conflicts had a natural, legal, or religious basis, depending on the circumstances.[66] Economic, legal, and religious categories were so tightly interwoven as to be inseparable.[67] Hence, "there was no possible position within such a society from which the economic basis of all social relations could be made conscious."[68]

The surviving literature of the early Empire validates Lukács judgment. Wherever something like a liberating counterideology appears, consciousness is mediated by a divine agent. An instructive example is the *Life of Aesop*, a genuine folk-book pervaded by an anti-Hellenic bias: here the claims of the educated elite to have a monopoly on wisdom are subjected to vulgar and witty criticism.[69]

Aesop is a mute, ugly, deformed slave, who, like other slaves, is beaten and tormented, and is powerless to retaliate.[70] The reversal of Aesop's fortunes is brought about not by resistance and revolt in concert with his fellow-slaves,[71] but by the goddess Isis and her daughters the Muses.[72] As a reward for Aesop's kindness to a priestess of Isis who has strayed from the highway and become lost, Aesop is granted the power of speech and the ability to conceive and elaborate tales.[73] The priestess petitions Isis: "O crown of the whole world, Isis of many names, have pity on this workman, who suffers and is pious, for the piety he has shown, not to me, O mistress, but to your appearance. And if you are unwilling to repay this man with a livelihood of many talents for what the other gods have taken from him, at least grant him the power of speech, for you have the power to bring back to light those things which have fallen into darkness."[74] The goddess subsequently appears to Aesop in a dream, and not only restores his voice, but asks each of her daughters, the nine Muses, to bestow on him something of her own talent too.[75] The author's point in making Isis's miracle the inaugural event in the *Life* is to assert the necessity of divine intervention in order to alleviate Aesop's plight. On this basis, the priestess of Isis makes her appeal: only with the help of the goddess can a poor workman, who labors under every disability, experience a liberated consciousness.

Obviously, Paul's epistle to the Romans construes awakening as mediated by a divine agent—the Messiah. So we may stipulate that the collective subjectivity whose awakening Paul summons is not an instance of class consciousness, as the latter is defined by orthodox Marxism.[76] Nor is it clear, in any case, that the Pauline *ekklēsia* was coextensive with a single class.[77] To be sure, the majority of believers in the communities founded by Paul were poor. Paul emphasizes "the abysmal poverty" (*hē kata bathous ptōcheia*) of the assemblies in Macedonia (2 Cor. 8:1–2).[78] Even in "wealthy Corinth," the majority of those who responded to the "calling" of Messiah Jesus were poor—uneducated, powerless, lowborn (1 Cor. 1:26).[79] Some, perhaps many, were slaves (1 Cor. 7:21; 12:13).[80] Yet, Crispus and Gaius at Corinth were persons of more than modest surplus resources.[81] And Paul commends Phoebe of Cenchreae as the "patroness of many" (*prostatis pollōn*) in Romans 16:1–2.[82] The formation of a community out of persons of different social classes would have necessitated a collective subjectivity that transcended class consciousness. Lukács judged a transcendence of immediate class interest for the sake of a totality to be impossible: "No class can do that—unless it is willing to abdicate its power freely."[83] Paul insists that precisely such an abdication of class interest is not only possible but necessary for a community that has grasped the full import of the event of the crucified Messiah.

Agamben deserves credit for having called attention to a passage in Marx that appears to be a secularization of the Pauline idea of a community whose collective subjectivity transcends class.[84] In "Contribution to the Critique of Hegel's Philosophy of Right," Marx attributes a redemptive function to the proletariat as the agent of a collective universalism:

> Where, then, is the possibility of . . . emancipation? Answer: In the formation of a class with radical chains, a class of civil society which is not a class of civil society, an estate which is the dissolution of all estates, a sphere which has a universal character by its universal suffering; . . . a sphere, finally, which cannot emancipate itself without emancipating itself from all other spheres of society, which, in a word, is the

complete loss of man, and hence can win itself only through the complete re-winning of man. This dissolution of society as a particular estate is the proletariat.[85]

Agamben comments: "The *ekklēsia* ... permits more than just one analogy with the Marxian proletariat. Just as he who is called is crucified with the Messiah and dies to the old world (Rom. 6:6) in order to be resuscitated to a new life (Rom. 8:11), so too is the proletariat only able to liberate itself through autosuppression. The 'complete loss' of man coincides with his complete redemption."[86]

But if we now ask what conclusion Agamben draws from this analogy, with respect to Paul's understanding of collective subjectivity, we are disappointed. The problem is not that Agamben questions whether one can really speak of a "classless society" in Paul.[87] Agamben knows that class conditions are null and void of meaning for Paul, even if Paul advises believers that "each should remain in the state in which he was called" (1 Cor. 7:20).[88] "Circumcision is nothing," Paul insists, "and uncircumcision is nothing" (1 Cor. 7:19). "Were you a slave when you were called?" Paul asks. "Never mind. For in the Lord, the one who was a slave when called is now a freedman of the Lord" (1 Cor. 7:21–22). Agamben knows that the Messiah has "redeemed" believers from every condition of existence (1 Cor. 7:23), embodying this insight in the paradoxical formula "the messianic vocation is the revocation of every vocation."[89]

The problem is that Agamben's notion of the collective subjectivity to which Paul summons seems to be devoid of content, that is, of identity: the worldly vocations are never replaced by a new vocation. Agamben insists: "The messianic vocation separates every *klēsis* from itself, engendering a tension within itself, without ever providing it with some other identity."[90] According to Agamben, the Pauline *ekklēsia* is a "remnant" produced by a "division of divisions," a "not-all" that dwells in "a zone of absolute indiscernibility between immanence and transcendence."[91] Agamben concludes: "The [messianic] people is neither the all nor the part, neither the majority nor the minority. Instead, it is that which can never coincide with itself, as all or as part, that which infinitely remains or resists each division. This remnant is the figure, or the substantiality assumed by a people in a decisive moment, and as such is the only real political subject."[92]

But of what sort of political action would Agamben's remnant be capable without a new identity, a new vocation? Perpetually in tension with itself, inhabiting a zone of indiscernibility between immanence and transcendence, the *ekklēsia*, as Agamben conceives it, seems to dwell within its vocation as an exile, in dispossession.[93] The political ethics appropriate to such a remnant would seem to be nonpossessive, kenotic waiting.[94] As a collectivity without identity, Agamben's *ekklēsia* is a space hollowed out within the power structure,[95] a space of messianic anticipation and perhaps even conspiratorial resistance. But as a collective immanence that is not fully aware of itself, Agamben's *ekklēsia* seems incapable of the "tiger's leap" of revolution.[96] One is tempted to characterize the spirit of passionate, messianic resignation that permeates Agamben's politics with Kafka's dictum: "[there is] plenty of hope, an infinite amount of hope—but not for us."[97]

In the end, the collective subjectivity to which Paul summons, and from which he demands the revolutionary practice of neighbor-love in the form of economic mutualism, seems better understood by Alain Badiou, who insists that Paul was advocating a collective universalism.[98] In the face of the collapse of Leninism, the party of the proletariat, and the socialist state, Badiou calls for "the evental opening of a new sequence of the communist hypothesis,"[99] which would consist in a "revolution of the mind,"[100] through the discovery of "a point that stands outside the temporality of the dominant order and what Lacan once called 'the service of wealth.'"[101] Toward the renewal of a collective consciousness, Badiou offers, as an experiment, a declaration: "There is only one world."[102] Badiou is fully aware that such an affirmation flies in the face of the "evidence" of capitalism's triumph all around us. Indeed, Badiou offers his affirmation as a deliberate counter to the "false" and "empty" universality of capitalism,[103] which has achieved its sovereignty by configuring the world as a homogeneous market of subjected and territorialized selves, so that nothing might impede the circulation of capital.[104] Badiou's utopian declaration, "There is only one world," "is not an objective conclusion; it is performative: we are deciding that this is how it will be for us."[105] Badiou concludes: "The political consequences of the axiom, 'there is only one world,' will work to consolidate what is universal in identities."[106]

Badiou's proposal has an uncanny similarity to the mature Paulinism of Romans 13:8–14, both in its commitment to the collective well-being of others and in its insistence that such a political commitment is possible only for those who "can connect to another temporality than that assigned to us by the dominant order."[107] Except that the collective subject that Paul seeks to awaken, and from whom he demands unconditional love, is not a *universal* subject, but a *singular* one, whose identity and ethics are determined by the Messiah. "We the many are one body in the Messiah" *(hoi polloi hen soma esmen en Christō)*, Paul instructs believers, "and according to one, members of one another *(to de kath' heis allēlōn melē)*" (Rom. 12:5).[108] The singular subject who confers unity, identity, and mission upon the many is the crucified Messiah, the one who died for all (2 Cor. 5:14), for the weak, for the ungodly (Rom. 5:6–8), for the nothings and nobodies (1 Cor. 1:26–28). Thus the "communitarian particularisms," against which Badiou rails as impediments to a universal truth,[109] are not erased in the Messiah, but embraced and affirmed. "The one who loves the other," the other as the very embodiment of difference, is the one who "fulfills the law" (Rom. 13:8b).[110]

We may summarize. By the time that Paul wrote his last epistle, his eschatology had undergone significant development—I would suggest, intensification. Paul no longer speaks of the *parousia*; whether he still believed in a "second coming" may be irrelevant. In any case, Paul had come to stake all upon the possibility of an "awakening." The awakening would occur when believers, who had been roused from the "sleep" imposed by the dominant order, grasped the full import of the messianic event for their present existence. This constellation is the "now time" that believers must discern. The awakened "sons [and daughters] of God" take full charge of their lives, casting aside the behaviors that have previously ensnared them. The awakened "sons [and daughters] of God" are the militants of the messianic event, capable of unplugging themselves from the patronage system and devoting themselves entirely to mutual love, expressed concretely in the practice of economic mutualism. In the broader context of Romans 12–15, Paul spells out the implications for life in the messianic community. Because the measure of communal identity and ethics is now the self-sacrificial love of Messiah Jesus, there is no longer any basis in law or custom for judging one another (Rom. 14). Radical hospitality, welcome without conditions, is the law of the new life in the Messiah: "Welcome one another," Paul concludes, "as the Messiah welcomed you, for the glory of God" (Rom. 15:7).[111]

The awakening to which Paul summons is a "revolution of the mind," to use the potent slogan of May 1968.[112] If the political consequences of the awakening are the practice of economic mutualism and radical hospitality within the community of believers, then must we speak of a revolution without a revolt? Or of a revolution that is indistinguishable, in its long-term consequences, from revolt?[113] In any case, it should be evident that the ethical commitment demanded by Paul in Romans 13:8–10, with its eschatological rationale in 13:11–14, is incompatible with the acquiescence and obedience to governmental authorities preached in Romans 13:1–7, as this passage has traditionally been interpreted.[114] Helmut Koester once questioned "if Rom. 13:1–7 is indeed Pauline and not a piece of Hellenistic-Jewish parenesis interpolated at a later date."[115] The thought and vocabulary of Romans 13:1–7 have more in common at key points with that of the quisling Josephus than with the language of Paul's authentic epistles.[116] If this passage is an interpolation, it has had a disastrous result: the interpolator has successfully diverted the attention of generations of interpreters from the revolutionary ethics and intense eschatology of Romans 13:8–14.[117] And there is worse: generations of the powerful have "cashed the blank check" that the interpolator wrote them by enjoining strict obedience to the governing authorities.[118]

7 | CODA

WHERE DOES IT stand today with Paul's summons to awakening? In my view, past eras instance several movements that are more than sporadic tremors of awakening: the monastic movement led by Francis of Assisi,[1] the struggle for social justice led by Martin Luther King.[2] Yet, for several decades now, a profound sleep has descended over most of the world because of the triumph of global capitalism. In a discourse that Giorgio Agamben delivered in March 2009 in Notre Dame Cathedral in the presence of the Bishop of Paris and other high-ranking clerics, he charged the church catholic with having forgotten its messianic calling.[3] Agamben asks: "Will the Church finally grasp the historical occasion and recover its messianic vocation?"[4] Then, Agamben warned: "If it does not, the risk is clear enough: it will be swept away by the disaster menacing every government and every institution on earth."[5] If I could name the danger that hangs over our present moment in late capitalism, it would be that the Judeo-Christian sense of social obligation embodied in the command to "love your neighbor" will be entirely obliterated by a resurgence of that structured inequality, with all its attendant cruelties, which was the basis of the political economy of the Roman Empire.[6]

At this dark moment, more than ever, we should recall that, according to Paul, the awakening occurs punctually, at the moment when night has advanced to its furthest point, when especially deep darkness holds sway just before the dawn (Rom. 13:12).

Notes

1. NEIGHBOR (A)

1. See the discussion in Hans Dieter Betz, *Galatians: A Commentary on Paul's Letter to the Churches in Galatia*, Hermeneia (Philadelphia: Fortress Press, 1979), 271–76.
2. Jacob Milgrom, *Leviticus 17–22: A New Translation with Introduction and Commentary*, Anchor Bible 3A (New York: Random House, 2000), 1319, 1346; Y. T. Radday, "Chiasmus in Hebrew Bible Narrative," in *Chiasmus in Antiquity: Structures, Analyses, Exegesis*, ed. J. Welch (Hildesheim: Gerstenberg Verlag, 1981), 89; Israel Knohl, *The Sanctuary of Silence: The Priestly Torah and the Holiness School* (Minneapolis: Fortress Press, 1995).
3. Robert Jewett, "Numerical Sequences in Paul's Letter to the Romans," in *Persuasive Artistry: Studies in New Testament Rhetoric in Honor of George A. Kennedy*, ed. D. F. Watson (Sheffield: JSOT Press, 1991), 227–45, here 234–35.
4. b Šabb. 31a. See the discussion in Hermann Strack and Paul Billerbeck, *Kommentar zum Neuen Testament aus Talmud und Midrasch* (Munich: Beck, 1922), 1:356–58; George Brockwell King, "The 'Negative' Golden Rule," *Journal of Religion* 8 (1928): 274–75; Wilhelm Bacher, *Die Agada der Tannaiten* (Berlin: de Gruyter, 1965), 1:4; W. D. Davies, *The Setting of the Sermon on the Mount* (Cambridge: Cambridge University Press, 1966), 401n2; Gerald Friedlander, *The Jewish Sources of the Sermon on the Mount* (New York: Ktav, 1969), 230–31; Jacob Neusner, *The Rabbinic Traditions About the Pharisees Before 70* (Leiden: Brill, 1971), 1:322–23; Kenneth Reinhard, "The Ethics of the Neighbor: Universalism, Particularism,

Exceptionalism," *Journal of Textual Reasoning* 4 (2005), http://etext.lib.virginia.edu/journals/tr/volume4/TR_04_01eol.html.

5. *t.Sotah* 9:11; *y.Ned.* 41c; *Gen. Rab.* 24:7; *Sipre* 200 on Lev. 19:18; see also *'Abot. R. Nat.* B 26. Cf. Andreas Nissen, *Gott und der Nächste im antiken Judentum* (Tübingen: Mohr Siebeck, 1974), 400–405; Reinhard Neudecker, "'And You Shall Love Your Neighbor as Yourself, I Am the Lord' (Lev. 19:18) in Jewish Interpretation," *Biblica* 73 (1992): 496–517.

6. Mark 12:31; Matthew 5:43; 19:19; 22:39; Luke 10:27; James 2:8; *Did.* 1:2; *Barn.* 19:5; *Ps-Clem. Hom.* 12.32; Justin *Dial.* 93.2–3; among others. See Davies, *Sermon on the Mount*, 370, 373, 402, 405n1; Victor P. Furnish, *The Love Command in the New Testament* (Nashville: Abingdon, 1972), passim; Klaus Berger, *Die Gesetzauslegung Jesu* (Neukirchen-Vluyn: Neukirchener Verlag, 1972), 80–83; Betz, *Galatians*, 276; W. D. Davies and Dale C. Allison, *Matthew 1–7*, ICC (London: T and T Clark, 1988), 548–64; Dale C. Allison, *Constructing Jesus: Memory, Imagination, and History* (Grand Rapids, Mich.: Baker Books, 2010), 359–60. See also Gerhard Lohfink, *Jesus of Nazareth: What He Wanted, Who He Was*, trans. Linda M. Maloney (Collegeville, Minn.: Liturgical Press, 2012), 192–93.

7. Betz, *Galatians*, 276; Oda Wischmeyer, "Das Gebot der Nächstenliebe bei Paulus: Eine traditionsgeschichtliche Untersuchung," *Biblische Zeitung* 30 (1986): 164, 168; James D. G. Dunn, *Romans 9–16*, Word Biblical Commentary 38b (Dallas: Word, 1988), 779; Dunn, "Paul's Knowledge of the Jesus Tradition: The Evidence of Romans," in *Christus Bezeugen: Für Wolfgang Trilling*, ed. K. Kertledge (Freiburg: Herder, 1990), 202; Michael Thompson, *Clothed with Christ: The Example and Teaching of Jesus in Romans 12,1–15,13* (Sheffield: Sheffield Academic Press, 1991), 132–40; Robert Jewett, *Romans: A Commentary*, Hermeneia (Minneapolis: Fortress Press, 2007), 813.

8. Jacob Taubes, *The Political Theology of Paul*, ed. Aleida Assmann with Jan Assmann, in conjunction with Horst Folkers, Wolf-Daniel Hartwich, and Christoph Schulte, trans. Dana Hollander (Stanford: Stanford University Press, 2004), 52–53. Taubes evidently regarded his discovery of Paul's reduction of the dual commandment as his most important exegetical insight, since it is discussed in both parts of the seminar (52–52, 55–56), and

resurfaces at the conclusion (92). Taubes's estimation of the importance of his contribution on this point has been validated by Kenneth Reinhard, "Paul and the Political Theology of the Neighbor," *soundandsignifier.com*, UCLA Center for Jewish Studies (May 2007), 1–32, esp. 17–19.

9. Taubes, *Political Theology of Paul*, 52–53.
10. See the discussion in W. D. Davies and Dale C. Allison, *Matthew 19–28*, ICC (London: T and T Clark, 1997), 235–49, esp. 240–45.
11. Taubes, *Political Theology of Paul*, 52–53.
12. In speaking of *kenōsis*, I am conflating Romans 5 with Philipians 2. Cf. Karl Kertledge, "Das Verständnis des Todes Jesu bei Paulus," in *Der Tod Jesu: Deutungen im Neuen Testament*, ed. J. Beutler (Freiburg: Herder, 1976), 114–36, esp. 123–24. Cf. Philippians 2:6–11, and the discussion in Günther Bornkamm, "Zum Verständnis des Christus-Hymnus, Phil. 2:6–11," in *Studien zu Antike und Urchristentum, Gesammlte Aufsätze* (Munich: Beck, 1951), 171–82; Ulrich B. Müller, *Der Brief des Paulus an die Philipper* (Leipzig: Evangelische Verlagsanstalt, 1993), 105; Samuel Vollenweider, "Der 'Raub' der Gottgleichheit: Ein religionsgeschichtlicher Vorschlag zu Phil. 2.6–11," *New Testament Studies* 45 (1999): 413–33; Vollenweider, "Die Metamorphose des Gottessohns: Zum epiphanialen Motivfeld in Phil. 2,6–8," in *Das Urchristentum in seiner literarischen Geschichte: Festgabe für Jürgen Becker zum 65. Geburtstag*, ed. U. Mell and U. B. Müller (Berlin: de Gruyter, 1999), 107–31; Christian Strecker, *Die liminale Theologie des Paulus: Zugänge zur paulinischen Theologie aus kultur-anthropologischer Perspektive* (Göttingen: Vandenhoeck und Ruprecht, 1999), 163–69.
13. See the discussion of this foundational text in Kertledge, "Verständnis des Todes Jesu bei Paulus," 116–24; Michael Wolter, *Rechtfertigung und zukünftiges Heil: Untersuchungen zu Röm 5,1–11* (Berlin: de Gruyter, 1978), 166–78; James D. G. Dunn, *Romans 1–8*, Word Biblical Commentary 38a (Dallas: Word, 1988), 1:254–60; Jewett, *Romans*, 355–68.
14. Sigmund Freud, *Der Mann Moses und die monotheistische Religion* (Frankfurt: Suhrkamp, 1964), 116–16; cited by Taubes, *Political Theology of Paul*, 92.
15. Taubes, *Political Theology of Paul*, 92.
16. Ibid., 82.

17. Ibid., 95.
18. Reinhard, "Paul and the Political Theology of the Neighbor," 21.
19. Milgrom, *Leviticus 17-22*, 1651-56; Neudecker, "And You Shall Love Your Neighbor."
20. Slavoj Žižek, Eric L. Santner, and Kenneth Reinhard, *The Neighbor: Three Inquiries in Political Theology* (Chicago: University of Chicago Press, 2005). On the importance of Taubes for the genesis of these inquiries, see Reinhard, "Paul and the Political Theology of the Neighbor," 2.
21. Sigmund Freud, *Civilization and Its Discontents*, trans. James Strachey (New York: Norton, 1989), 66-69; cited in Žižek, Santner, and Reinhard, *The Neighbor*, 1.
22. Freud, *Civilization and Its Discontents*, 67; cited in Žižek, Santner, and Reinhard, *The Neighbor*, 2.
23. Freud, *Civilization and Its Discontents*, 68; cited in Žižek, Santner, and Reinhard, *The Neighbor*, 2.
24. Freud, *Civilization and Its Discontents*, 69; cited in Žižek, Santner, and Reinhard, *The Neighbor*, 2.
25. Kenneth Reinhard, "Toward a Political Theology of the Neighbor," in Žižek, Santner, and Reinhard, *The Neighbor*, 11-75, here 13-14, 50-59.
26. Ibid., 13-14, 61-67.
27. Ibid., 45-46, 71-74.
28. Ibid., 73.
29. Eric L. Santner, "Miracles Happen: Benjamin, Rosenzweig, Freud, and the Matter of the Neighbor," in Žižek, Santner, and Reinhard, *The Neighbor*, 76-133.
30. Santner, "Miracles Happen," 91-92, referencing Jacques Lacan, *The Seminar of Jacques Lacan*, book 11, *The Four Fundamental Concepts of Psychoanalysis*, trans. Alan Sheridan (New York: Norton, 1981), 214; and Jean Laplanche, *New Foundations for Psychoanalysis*, trans. David Macey (Oxford: Basil Blackwell, 1989), 130.
31. Santner, "Miracles Happen," 92, referencing Jean Laplanche, *Essays on Otherness*, ed. John Fletcher (London: Routledge, 1999), 80.
32. Santner, "Miracles Happen," 92.
33. Ibid., 125.

34. Ibid., 132–33.
35. Ibid., 133.
36. Ibid., referencing Franz Rosenzweig, *Der Mensch und sein Werk*, in *Gesammelte Schriften*, ed. Reinhold Mayer and Annemarie Mayer (Dordrecht: Martonus Nijhoff, 1984), 1:2:770–71.
37. Santner, "Miracles Happen," 133.
38. Slavoj Žižek, "Neighbors and Other Monsters: A Plea for Ethical Violence," in Žižek, Santner, and Reinhard, *The Neighbor*, 134–90.
39. Ibid., 142–57.
40. Ibid., 158–69.
41. According to F. C. Baur, "Die Christuspartei in der korinthischen Gemeinde, der Gegensatz des petrinischen und paulinischen Christentums in der ältesten Kirche, der Apostel Petrus in Rom," *Tübinger Zeitschrift für Theologie* 4 (1831): 61–206, here 114–16; Baur, *Paulus, der Apostel Jesu Christi: Sein Leben und Wirken, sein Briefe und seine Lehre, ein Beitrag zu einer kritischen Geschichte des Urchristentums* (Stuttgart: Becher und Müller, 1845), with a second edition published in 1866; followed by Adolf Hilgenfeld, *Judentum und Judenchristentum: Eine Nachlese zur Ketzergeschichte des Urchristentums* (Leipzig: Fues, 1886); Hilgenfeld, "Der Clemens-Roman," *Zeitschrift für wissenschaftliche Theologie* 49 (1906): 66–133. See the discussion in Gerd Lüdemann, *Paulus, der Heidenapostel*, vol. 2, *Antipaulinismus im frühen Christentum* (Göttingen: Vandenhoeck und Ruprecht, 1983), 15, 15n12, 17n24, 41.
42. Žižek, "Neighbors and Other Monsters," 189.
43. Ibid., 187.
44. Ibid., 190.
45. Ibid., 188–89.
46. Ibid., 190. Elsewhere, Žižek seems to express a rather different perspective on the relationship between Judaism and Christianity: see Žižek, *The Puppet and the Dwarf: The Perverse Core of Christianity* (Cambridge, Mass.: MIT Press, 2003), 3–6, 108–12, 133–36. Žižek would doubtless explain that the difference is only due to a parallactic shift of perspective.
47. Jewett, *Romans*, 817. Similarly, Otto Michel, *Der Brief an die Römer*, Kritisch-exegetischer Kommentar 4 (Göttingen: Vandenhoeck und

Ruprecht, 1978), 412; C. E. B. Cranfield, *A Critical and Exegetical Commentary on the Epistle to the Romans*, International Critical Commentary (Edinburgh: T and T Clark, 1979), 2:679; Franz-Josef Ortkemper, *Leben aus dem Glauben: Christliche Grundhaltungen nach Römer 12–13* (Münster: Aschendorff, 1980), 132; Dunn, *Romans 9–16*, 784–85; Joseph A. Fitzmyer, *Romans: A New Translation with Introduction and Commentary*, Anchor Bible 33 (New York: Doubleday, 1993), 681–82; Peter Stuhlmacher, *Paul's Letter to the Romans: A Commentary*, trans. S. J. Hafemann (Louisville, Ky.: Westminster John Knox, 1994), 212.

48. Giorgio Agamben, *The Time That Remains: A Commentary on the Letter to the Romans*, trans. Patricia Daley (Stanford: Stanford University Press, 2005), 2–3 and passim.

49. Alain Badiou, *Saint Paul: The Foundation of Universalism*, trans. Ray Brassier (Stanford: Stanford University Press, 2003), 55–64 and passim.

50. Taubes, *Political Theology of Paul*, 53.

51. Ibid., 1.

52. Ibid., 53–54. Perhaps Taubes was drawn to 1 Corinthians 7:29–31 by Martin Heidegger's comments on this passage in his seminar of the early 1920s: see Martin Heidegger, *Einleitung in die Phänomenologie der Religion*, in *Gesamtausgabe*, ed. Matthias Jung (Frankfurt: Klostermann, 1995), 60:1:117–19. In any case, subsequent interpreters have focused on 1 Corinthians 7:29–31 in seeking to understand Pauline eschatology, to the detriment of Romans 13:11–14: for example, Agamben, *The Time That Remains*, 23–43; Žižek, *The Puppet and the Dwarf*, 111–12; Žižek, *The Fragile Absolute, or, Why Is the Christian Legacy Worth Fighting For?* (New York: Verso, 2000), 129; Travis Kroeker, "Living 'As If Not': Messianic Becoming or the Practice of Nihilism?," in *Paul, Philosophy, and the Theopolitical Vision: Critical Engagements with Agamben, Badiou, Žižek, and Others*, ed. Douglas Harink (Eugene, Oreg.: Cascade Books, 2010), 37–63, esp. 59–63.

53. Especially as mediated by the essays and responses in Stephen D. Moore and Mayra Rivera, eds., *Planetary Loves: Spivak, Postcoloniality, and Theology* (New York: Fordham University Press, 2011).

54. Julia Kristeva, *Strangers to Ourselves* (New York: Columbia University Press, 1994).

55. On the context and composition of these writings, see J. Schüpphaus, *Die Psalmen Salomos: Ein Zeugnis Jerusalemer Theologie und Frömmigkeit in der Mitte des vorchristlichen Jahrhunderts* (Leiden: Brill, 1977); Robert B. Wright, "Psalms of Solomon," in *The Old Testament Pseudepigrapha*, ed. James H. Charlesworth (Garden City, N.Y.: Doubleday, 1985), 2:639–72; Wright, *The Psalms of Solomon: A Critical Edition of the Greek Text* (New York: T and T Clark, 2007); Kenneth Atkinson, "Herod the Great, Sosius, and the Siege of Jerusalem in Psalms of Solomon 17," *Novum Testamentum* 38 (1996): 313–22; Atkinson, *I Cried to the Lord: A Study of the Psalms of Solomon's Historical Background and Social Setting* (Leiden: Brill, 2004); Marinus de Jonge, *Studies on the Testaments of the Twelve Patriarchs* (Leiden: Brill, 1979); de Jonge, *Pseudepigrapha of the Old Testament as Part of Christian Literature: The Case of the Testaments of the Twelve Patriarchs* (Leiden: Brill, 2003); James L. Kugel, *The Ladder of Jacob: Ancient Interpretations of the Biblical Story of Jacob and His Children* (Princeton: Princeton University Press, 2006).

56. For example, Seneca, *Hercules Furens*. See the discussion in John G. Fitch and S. McElduff, "Construction of the Self in Senecan Drama," *Mnemosyne* 55 (2002): 18–40; Emma Jane Scott, "The Poetics of Sleep: Representing Dreams and Sleep in Latin Literature and Roman Art" (PhD diss., UCLA, 2005); Basil Dufallo, *The Ghosts of the Past: Latin Literature, the Dead, and Rome's Transition to a Principate* (Columbus: Ohio State University Press, 2007).

57. For example, Ps.-Plato *Cleitophon* 407B–408C; Epictetus *Diss.* 2.20.10–15; *Corp. herm.*1.15.23; *Corp. herm.* 13.4. See the discussion in Simon Roelof Slings, *A Commentary on the Platonic Clitophon* (Amsterdam: Academische Pers, 1981); William C. Grese, *Corpus Hermeticum XIII and Early Christian Literature* (Leiden: Brill, 1979).

2. *KAIROS* (B)

1. On the difficulty of the phrase, see Fréderic Godet, *Commentary on St. Paul's Epistle to the Romans* (Grand Rapids, Mich.: Kregel, 1977), 448–49; James D. G. Dunn, *Romans 9–16*, Word Biblical Commentary 38b (Dallas: Word, 1988), 785; Joseph A. Fitzmyer, *Romans: A New Translation*

with *Introduction and Commentary*, Anchor Bible 33 (New York: Doubleday, 1993), 682; Robert Jewett, *Romans: A Commentary*, Hermeneia (Minneapolis: Fortress Press, 2007), 818–19. The phrase *kai touto* (and this) is described as "emphatic" in F. Blass and A. Debrunner, *A Greek Grammar of the New Testament and Other Early Christian Literature*, trans. and rev. R. W. Funk (Chicago: University of Chicago Press, 1961), §553.9, and should be rendered "and at that" or "and especially" §290.

2. So, Karl Barth, *The Epistle to the Romans*, 6th ed., trans. Edwin C. Hoskyns (Oxford: Oxford University Press, 1968), 497–98; Franz-Josef Leenhardt, *The Epistle of Saint Paul to the Romans: A Commentary*, trans. H. Knight (London: Lutterworth, 1961), 338; Heinrich Schlier, *Der Römerbrief*, Herders theologischer Kommentar zum Neuen Testament 6 (Freiburg: Herder, 1977), 389; Otto Michel, *Der Brief an die Römer*, KEK 4 (Göttingen: Vandenhoeck und Ruprecht, 1978), 413; Johannes P. Louw, *A Semantic Discourse Analysis of Romans* (Pretoria: University of Pretoria Press, 1979), 2.125; Ulrich Wilckens, *Der Brief an die Römer, 3. Teilband Röm 12–16*, Evangelisch-katholischer Kommentar (Zürich: Benziger Verlag, 1982), 75; Fitzmyer, *Romans*, 682; Douglas J. Moo, *The Epistle to the Romans*, New International Commentary on the New Testament (Grand Rapids, Mich.: Eerdmans, 1996), 817, 819.

3. Schlier, *Der Römerbrief*, 395–97, suggests that a baptismal hymn is quoted in 13:11–12, while Jewett, *Romans*, 817–18, suggests an Agape hymn. Schlier and Jewett regard 13:11c *(nun gar egguteron hēmōn hē sōtēria ē hote episteusamen)* as an explanatory addition to the hymn by Paul.

4. The participle *eidotes* (knowing) in 13:11a clearly takes "the *kairos*" (*ton kairon*) as its object, not *touto* (this), as Jewett, *Romans*, 818, suggests: "The expression *touto eidotes* ("knowing this") is used in an indicative sense, since it does not follow a finite verb in this sentence." Note the absence of *hoti* (that) after *eidotes*, which, in other cases (for example, 1 Cor. 15:58; 2 Cor. 4:14; Gal. 2:16; Rom. 5:3; 6:9), signals that quoted material follows.

5. Jewett, *Romans*, 819, referencing Jörg Baumgarten, *"kairos,"* *Exegetical Dictionary of the New Testament* 2 (1991): 333. Similarly, Fitzmyer, *Romans*, 682; Peter Stuhlmacher, *Paul's Letter to the Romans: A Commentary*,

trans. S. J. Hafemann (Louisville, Ky.: Westminster John Knox, 1994), 212–13; Moo, *Romans*, 819–20; Luke Timothy Johnson, *Reading Romans: A Literary and Theological Commentary*, Reading the New Testament Series (New York: Crossroad, 1997), 206.

6. For example, 2 *Apoc. Bar.* 85.10. See the discussion of apocalyptic views in Gerhard Dautzenberg, "Was bleibt von der Naherwartung? Zu Röm 13:11–14," in *Biblische Randbemerkungen: Schülerfestschrift Rudolf Schnackenburg*, ed. H. Merklein and J. Lange (Würzburg: Echter, 1974), 361–74; Franz-Josef Ortkemper, *Leben aus dem Glauben: Christliche Grundhaltungen nach Römer 12–13* (Münster: Aschendorff, 1980), 133; Anton Vögtle, "Röm 13:11–14 und die 'Nah'-Erwartung," in *Rechtfertigung*, ed. J. Friedrich (Tübingen: Mohr Siebeck, 1976), 557–73.

7. G. L. Davenport, "The 'Anointed of the Lord' in Psalms of Solomon 17," in *Ideal Figures in Ancient Judaism*, ed. John J. Collins and G. W. Nickelsburg (Chico: Scholars Press, 1980), 67–92; Robert B. Wright, "Psalms of Solomon," in *The Old Testament Pseudepigrapha*, ed. James H. Charlesworth (Garden City, N.Y.: Doubleday, 1985), 2:643–47, 667–68; Marinus de Jonge, "Expectation of the Future in the Psalms of Solomon," *Neotestamentica* 23 (1989): 93–117; Craig A. Evans, "Messianic Hopes and Messianic Figures in Late Antiquity," *Journal of Greco-Roman Christianity and Judaism* 3 (2006): 9–40, esp. 20–22; Andrew Chester, *Messiah and Exaltation: Jewish Messianic and Visionary Traditions and New Testament Christology* (Tübingen: Mohr Siebeck, 2007), 340–44.

8. Wright, "Psalms of Solomon," 643–47; Chester, *Messiah and Exaltation*, 341–44; Evans, "Messianic Hopes and Messianic Figures," 21–22.

9. H. W. Hollander and M. de Jonge, *The Testaments of the Twelve Patriarchs* (Leiden: Brill, 1985), 179–82; Marinus de Jonge, *Pseudepigrapha of the Old Testament as Part of Christian Literature: The Case of the Testaments of the Twelve Patriarchs* (Leiden: Brill, 2003), 124–40.

10. Émile Puech, "Fragments d'un apocrypha de Lévi et le personnage eschatologique: 4QTestLévi (?) et 4QAJa," in *The Madrid Qumran Conference: Proceedings of the International Congress on the Dead Sea Scrolls*, ed. J. Trebolle Barrera and L. Vegas Montaner (Leiden: Brill, 1992), 2:449–501; James C. Vanderkam, "Messianism and Apocalypticism," in *The*

Continuum History of Apocalypticism, ed. Bernard McGinn, John J. Collins, and Stephen J. Stein (New York: Continuum, 2003), 120-21; George J. Brooke, "The Apocryphon of Levi (?) and the Messianic Servant High Priest," in *The Dead Sea Scrolls and the New Testament* (Minneapolis: Fortress Press, 2005), 140-57; Michael A. Knibb, "Messianism in the Pseudepigrapha in the Light of the Scrolls," in *Essays on the Book of Enoch and Other Early Jewish Texts and Traditions* (Leiden: Brill, 2009), 307-26; John J. Collins, *The Scepter and the Star: Messianism in Light of the Dead Sea Scrolls* (Grand Rapids, Mich.: Eerdmans, 2010), 89-93.

11. The literature on the Synoptic Apocalypse is immense, and scholars differ regarding its occasion: the Caligula crisis, Nero's persecution, the Jewish war, or a persecution of Christians at the time of Vespasian. For an evaluation of the literature, see Rudolf Pesch, *Naherwartungen: Tradition und Redaktion in Mk 13* (Düsseldorf: Patmos, 1968), 19-47; Egon Brandenburger, *Markus 13 und die Apokalyptik* (Göttingen: Vandenhoeck und Ruprecht, 1984), 21-42. See further G. Hölscher, "Der Ursprung der Apokalypse Markus 13," *Theologische Blätter* 12 (1933): 193-202; Lars Hartman, *Prophecy Interpreted: The Formation of Some Jewish Apocalyptic Texts and the Eschatological Discourse Mark 13 Par.* (Lund: Gleerup, 1966); Luise Schottroff, "Die Gegenwart in der Apokalyptik der synoptischen Evangelien," in *Apocalypticism in the Mediterranean World and the Near East: Proceedings of the International Colloquium on Apocalypticism, Uppsala, August 12-17, 1979*, ed. David Hellholm (Tübingen: Mohr Siebeck, 1989), 707-28; Martin Hengel, "Entstehungszeit und Situation des Markusevangeliums," in *Markus-Philologie: Historische, literaturgeschichtliche und stilistische Untersuchungen zum zweiten Evangelium*, ed. H. Cancik (Tübingen: Mohr Siebeck, 1984), 1-45; Adela Yarbro Collins, "The Eschatological Discourse of Mark 13," in *The Four Gospels 1992*, ed. F. Van Segbroeck (Leuven: Leuven University Press, 1992), 2:1125-40; Gerd Theissen, "The Great Eschatological Discourse and the Threat to the Temple in 40 C.E.," in *The Gospels in Context: Social and Political History in the Synoptic Tradition* (London: T and T Clark, 2004), 125-65.

12. On the sayings in Mark 13 announcing the coming of Jesus as the Son of Man at a future time that no one knows, see Helmut Koester, *Introduction*

to the New Testament, vol. 2, History and Literature of Early Christianity, 2nd ed. (Berlin: de Gruyter, 2000), 153–54; cf. G. R. Beasley-Murray, Jesus and the Last Days: The Interpretation of the Olivet Discourse (Peabody: Hendrickson, 1993); John T. Carroll, "The Parousia of Jesus in the Synoptic Gospels and Acts," in The Return of Jesus in Early Christianity, ed. John T. Carroll (Peabody: Hendrickson, 2000), 9–13.

13. Cf. Luke 21:25–28; Hebrews 10:25; James 5:8; 1 Peter 4:7; see the discussion in Dautzenberg, "Was Bleibt von der Naherwartung?," 361–74; Ortkemper, *Leben aus dem Glauben*, 133; Vögtle, "Röm 13:11–14 und die 'Nah'-Erwartung," 557–73; Alexandra R. Brown, "Paul and the Parousia," in Carroll, *The Return of Jesus in Early Christianity*, 47–76; Dunn, *Romans 9–16*, 786–87; Jewett, *Romans*, 821, with almost all commentators.

14. Gustav Stählin, *"nun," Theological Dictionary of the New Testament* 4 (1967): 1120; similarly, Michel, *Der Brief an die Römer*, 414; Dunn, *Romans 9–16*, 786; Jewett, *Romans*, 820.

15. Walter Bauer, *A Greek-English Lexicon of the New Testament and Other Early Christian Literature*, 3rd ed., rev. and ed. Frederick William Danker (Chicago: University of Chicago Press, 2000), 681; cf. Schlier, *Der Römerbrief*, 396; Dunn, *Romans 9–16*, 786.

16. Dunn, *Romans 9–16*, 786; Jewett, *Romans*, 820.

17. Heinz Giesen, *"hōra," Exegetical Dictionary of the New Testament* 3 (1993): 508. Cf. C. E. B. Cranfield, *A Critical and Exegetical Commentary on the Epistle to the Romans*, ICC (Edinburgh: T and T Clark, 1979), 2:681–82; Moo, *Epistle to the Romans*, 818, 822.

18. Gerhard Delling, *"kairos," Theological Dictionary of the New Testament* 3 (1965): 460.

19. Jewett, *Romans*, 819n23, citing Plato *Prot*. 361e6: *nun d' hōra ēdē kat' ep' allo ti trepesthai* (But now it's past time to turn to another matter); Arrian *Tact*. 33.6.4: *hōra ēdē legein* (it is past time to speak); see also Polybius 10.40.12; Lucian *Pseudol*. 32.12; Pausanias *Graec. descr*. 9.13.5. Cf. Gerhard Delling, *"hōra," Theological Dictionary of the New Testament* 9 (1974): 675–81.

20. Cranfield, *Epistle to the Romans*, 2:680–81; Dunn, *Romans 9–16*, 785; Jewett, *Romans*, 819.

21. For *episteusamen* as an ingressive aorist, see Blass and Debrunner, *Greek Grammar*, §331; C. F. D. Moule, *An Idiom Book of New Testament Greek* (Cambridge: Cambridge University Press, 1953), 10–11; Godet, *Commentary on Romans*, 450; Cranfield, *Epistle to the Romans*, 681; Michel, *Der Brief an die Römer*, 414; Dunn, *Romans 9–16*, 786; Jewett, *Romans*, 821. For Pauline other uses of the aorist of *pisteuō* to indicate the act of commitment that marked entrance into the messianic community, see 1 Corinthians 3:5; 15:2, 11; Galatians 2:16.

22. Evald Lövestam, *Spiritual Wakefulness in the New Testament* (Lund: Gleerup, 1963), 33; Anton Grabner-Haider, *Paraklese und Eschatologie bei Paulus* (Münster: Aschendorff, 1968), 84–85; Vögtle, "Röm 13:11–14 und die 'Nah'-Erwartung," 566; Ortkemper, *Leben aus dem Glauben*, 136, 138–39; Michael Thompson, *Clothed with Christ: The Example and Teaching of Jesus in Romans 12,1–15,13* (Sheffield: Sheffield Academic Press, 1991), 143–44.

23. Giorgio Agamben, *The Time That Remains: A Commentary on the Letter to the Romans*, trans. Patricia Daley (Stanford: Stanford University Press, 2005), 59–87; see the discussion in Ryan L. Hansen, "Messianic or Apocalyptic? Engaging Agamben on Paul and Politics," in *Paul, Philosophy, and the Theopolitical Vision: Critical Engagements with Agamben, Badiou, Žižek, and Others*, ed. Douglas Harink (Eugene, Oreg.: Cascade Books, 2010), 198–223; Douglas Harink, "Time and Politics in Four Commentaries on Romans," in Harink, *Paul, Philosophy, and the Theopolitical Vision*, 304–11.

24. Agamben, *The Time That Remains*, 62.

25. Ibid., 71. See the classic statement of this insight by Albert Schweitzer, *The Mysticism of Paul the Apostle*, trans. William Montgomery (Baltimore: Johns Hopkins University Press, 1998), 99: "While other believers held that the finger of the world-clock was touching on the beginning of the coming hour and were waiting for the stroke that should announce this, Paul told them that it had already passed beyond the point, and that they had failed to hear the striking of the hour, which in fact struck at the Resurrection of Jesus." See further Rudolf Bultmann, *The Theology of the New Testament* (New York: Scribner's, 1951), 1:278–29: Christ's death and res-

urrection was, for Paul, "the eschatological event by which God ended the old course of the world and introduced a new aeon... what for the Jews is a *matter of hope* is for Paul a *present reality*—or better, is also a present reality" (emphasis original). Cf. M. C. de Boer, "Paul and Apocalyptic Eschatology," in McGinn, Collins, and Stein, *The Continuum History of Apocalypticism*, 166–81, esp. 173.

26. Agamben, *The Time That Remains*, 62; see the discussion in Gordon Zerbe, "On the Exigency of a Messianic Ecclesia: An Engagement with Philosophical Readers of Paul," in Harink, *Paul, Philosophy, and the Theopolitical Vision*, 260.
27. Agamben, *The Time That Remains*, 63.
28. Ibid., 64.
29. Ibid., 65–68; see Hansen, "Messianic or Apocalyptic?," 202–3.
30. Agamben, *The Time That Remains*, 65.
31. Ibid., 65–66.
32. Ibid., 67.
33. Ibid., 69.
34. Ibid., 64, emphasis mine.
35. Ibid.
36. Ibid., 62; similarly, Giorgio Agamben, *The Church and the Kingdom*, trans. Leland de la Durantaye (London: Seagull Books, 2012), 13. The images reflect the participle *sunestalmenos* used by Paul in 1 Corinthians 7:29 to describe the *kairos*.
37. Agamben, *The Time That Remains*, 71.
38. Ibid., referencing Franz Kafka, *Hochzeitsvorbereitung auf dem Lande und andere Prosa aus dem Nachlass*, vol. 8, *Gesammelte Werke*, ed. Max Brod (Frankfurt: Fischer, 1966), 90, and an Islamic text cited in Paul Casanova, *Mohammed et la fin du Monde* (Paris: Geuthner, 1911), 69.
39. Agamben, *The Time That Remains*, 67, 71.
40. Ibid., 67.
41. Ibid., 65–67.
42. For Paul's proclamation of the messianic event as antiphilosophical, see esp. 1 Corinthians 1:18—2:16, with the assessment of Alain Badiou, *Saint Paul: The Foundation of Universalism*, trans. Ray Brassier (Stanford:

Stanford University Press, 2003), 17, 46–54. Cf. L. L. Welborn, *Paul, the Fool of Christ: A Study of 1 Corinthians 1–4 in the Comic-Philosophic Tradition* (London: T and T Clark, 2005).
43. Agamben, *The Time That Remains*, 69.
44. Ibid.
45. Ibid., 67.
46. Ibid., 63, 70–71.
47. Ibid., 69.
48. Ibid.
49. On the influence of the tradition of Jesus's sayings upon Romans 13:11–14, see David Wenham, "Paul and the Synoptic Apocalypse," in *Studies of History and Tradition in the Four Gospels*, ed. R. T. France and D. Wenham (Sheffield: JSOT Press, 1981), 345–75; Wenham, *The Rediscovery of Jesus' Eschatological Discourse* (Sheffield: JSOT Press, 1984), 116, 325–26; Thompson, *Clothed with Christ*, 141–60. Especially suggestive are the similarities between Romans 13:11–14 and the parable of the Night Watchers in Mark 13:33–37, the nucleus of which goes back to the historical Jesus; see C. H. Dodd, *The Parables of the Kingdom* (New York: Scribner's, 1961), 127–32; Luise Schottroff, *The Parables of Jesus* (Minneapolis: Fortress Press, 2006), 124–29.
50. On *eggizō* and *eggus* in expressions of the nearness of the decisive day, the coming of the kingdom of God, see Herbert Preisker, "*eggus, ktl.*," *Theological Dictionary of the New Testament* 2 (1964): 331; Detlev Dormeyer, "*eggizō*," *Exegetical Dictionary of the New Testament* 1 (1991): 370.
51. A. L. Moore, *The Parousia in the New Testament* (Leiden: Brill, 1966), 122n1; Cranfield, *Epistle to the Romans*, 2:682; Michel, *Der Römerbrief*, 414; Thompson, *Clothed with Christ*, 146–47; Dunn, *Romans 9–16*, 786; Jewett, *Romans*, 822. On Mark 1:15 and Paul, see Ernst Lohmeyer, *Das Evangelium des Markus*, Kritisch-exegetischer Kommentar über das Neue Testament (Göttingen: Vandenhoeck und Ruprecht, 1967), 30. On Jesus's proclamation of the arrival of God's kingdom in Q, see Heinz Schürmann, "Das Zeugnis der Redenquelle für die Basileia-Verkündigung Jesu: Eine traditionsgeschichtliche Untersuchung," in *Logia: Les Paroles de Jésus—The Sayings of Jesus*, ed. Joëlm Delobel (Leuven: Leuven Univer-

sity Press, 1982), 121–200; Helmut Koester, "The Sayings of Q and Their Image of Jesus," in *Sayings of Jesus: Canonical and Non-Canonical: Essays in Honor of Tjitze Baarda*, ed. William L. Petersen, Johan S. Vos, and H. J. de Jonge (Leiden: Brill, 1997), 137–54; James M. Robinson, "Jesus' Sayings About God Reigning," in *Jesus According to the Earliest Witness* (Minneapolis: Fortress Press, 2007), 120–28. See further Helmut Merklein, *Jesu Botschaft von der Gottesherrschaft: Eine Skizze* (Stuttgart: Katholisches Bibelwerk, 1989), 23. On the meaning of *basileia* in Q and how the term should be translated, see now Giovanni Bazzana, "*Basileia*—the Q Concept of Kingship in Light of Documentary Papyri," in *Light from the East: Papyrologische Kommentare zum Neuen Testament*, ed. Peter Arzt-Grabner and Christina M. Kreinecker (Wiesbaden: Harrassowitz Verlag, 2010), 153–68.

52. Lohmeyer, *Das Evangelium des Markus*, 30.
53. Vögtle, "Röm 13:11–14 und die 'Nah'-Erwartung," 564; Jewett, *Romans*, 821.
54. Norman Perrin, *The Kingdom of God in the Teaching of Jesus* (Philadelphia: Westminster, 1963); G. R. Beasley-Murray, *Jesus and the Kingdom of God* (Grand Rapids, Mich.: Eerdmans, 1986); Dale C. Allison, "The Eschatology of Jesus," in McGinn, Collins, and Stein, *The Continuum History of Apocalypticism*, 139–65; Allison, *Constructing Jesus: Memory, Imagination, and History* (Grand Rapids, Mich.: Baker Books, 2010), 31, 91, 112, 201.
55. Johannes Weiss, *Die Predigt Jesu vom Reich Gottes* (Göttingen: Vandenhoeck und Ruprecht, 1892); translated into English as *Jesus' Proclamation of the Kingdom of God* (Philadelphia: Fortress Press, 1971); Albert Schweitzer, *The Quest of the Historical Jesus: A Critical Study of Its Progress from Reimarus to Wrede* (New York: Macmillan, 1968).
56. C. H. Dodd, *The Parables of the Kingdom* (New York: Scribner's, 1961); Dodd, *The Founder of Christianity* (New York: Scribner's, 1970); John A. T. Robinson, *Jesus and His Coming* (Philadelphia: Westminster, 1979), 36–82.
57. John Dominic Crossan, *In Parables: The Challenge of the Historical Jesus* (New York: Harper and Row, 1973); Crossan, *The Historical Jesus: The Life of a Mediterranean Jewish Peasant* (San Francisco: Harper, 1991); Norman Perrin, *Jesus and the Language of the Kingdom* (Philadelphia: Fortress

Press, 1976); John P. Meier, *A Marginal Jew: Rethinking the Historical Jesus*, vol. 2, *Mentor, Message, and Miracles* (New York: Doubleday, 1994).

58. James L. Kugel, *The Idea of Biblical Poetry: Parallelism and Its History* (Baltimore: Johns Hopkins University Press, 1998); James L. Bailey, *Literary Forms in the New Testament: A Handbook* (Louisville, Ky.: Westminster John Knox, 1992), 162–63.

59. Paul Joüon, "Notes philologiques sur les Evangiles," *Recherches de science religieuse* 17 (1927): 537–40; cf. Joel Marcus, "'The Time Has Been Fulfilled!' (Mark 1:15)," in *Apocalyptic and the New Testament: Essays in Honor of J. Louis Martyn*, ed. Joel Marcus and Marion L. Soards (Sheffield: JSOT Press, 1989), 49–68; Dale C. Allison, *Jesus of Nazareth: Millenarian Prophet* (Minneapolis: Augsburg Fortress, 1998), 59–60, 121; Ben F. Meyer, "How Jesus Charged Language with Meaning: A Study in Rhetoric," in *Authenticating the Words of Jesus*, ed. Bruce D. Chilton and Craig A. Evans (Leiden: Brill, 1999), 81–96, esp. 90. As is well known, Rudolf Bultmann regarded Mark 1:15 as "a secondary formulation . . . which might very well derive from Mark himself." Bultmann, *The History of the Synoptic Tradition*, trans. John Marsh (New York: Harper and Row, 1963), 118; similarly, Werner H. Kelber, *The Kingdom in Mark* (Philadelphia: Fortress Press, 1974), 9; John Dominic Crossan, *In Fragments: The Aphorisms of Jesus* (San Francisco: Harper and Row, 1983), 56.

60. Bauer, *A Greek-English Lexicon*, 828, s.v., *plēroō* 2. Cf. Delling, "*kairos*," 460.

61. Koester, *Introduction to the New Testament*, 2:152; see further Paul Hoffmann, *Studien zur Theologie der Logienquelle* (Münster: Aschendorff, 1982); Dieter Zeller, *Kommentar zur Logienquelle* (Stuttgart: Katholisches Bibelwerk, 1984).

62. On the imminent eschatology of Jesus, see Erich Grässer, *Die Naherwartung Jesu* (Stuttgart: Katholisches Bibelwerk, 1973).

63. Émile Benveniste, *Problems in General Linguistics*, trans. Mary Elizabeth Meek (Miami: University of Miami Press, 1971), 217–20; cited and discussed by Agamben, *The Time That Remains*, 66–67.

64. For this conception of time, see Walter Benjamin, "Über den Begriff der Geschichte," in *Gesammelte Schriften*, vol. 1.2, ed. Rolf Tiedemann and

Hermann Schweppenhäuser (Frankfurt: Suhrkamp, 1974), 693–704; translated into English as "Theses on the Philosophy of History," in *Illuminations*, ed. Hannah Arendt, trans. Harry Zohn (Glasgow: Fontana/Collins, 1979), 255–66.

65. As illustrated, for example, by the parable of the Harvest Time in Mark 4:26–29, the parable of the Night Watchers in Mark 13:28–37, and the parable of the Feast in Luke 14:16–24/Matthew 22:1–10/Gospel of Thomas 64. See the interpretations of these parables by C. H. Dodd, *The Parables of the Kingdom* (New York: Scribner's, 1961); Crossan, *In Parables*; Schottroff, *The Parables of Jesus*.

66. Scholars of early Christianity conventionally cite the Sayings Gospel Q according to Luke, reflecting the consensus that, in most cases, Luke preserves the Q material more faithfully than Matthew; see Helmut Koester, *Ancient Christian Gospels: Their History and Development* (Harrisburg: Trinity Press, 1990), 128–33.

67. See already Schweitzer, *The Mysticism of Paul the Apostle*, 99.

68. On the modification of Jewish apocalyptic eschatology brought about by Paul's conviction that the messianic event had already occurred, see ibid., 90–100; Bultmann, *Theology of the New Testament*, 1:278–79; cf. de Boer, "Paul and Apocalyptic Eschatology," 173–81.

3. AWAKENING (C)

1. For example, Ps.-Plato *Cleitophon* 407B–408C; Epictetus *Diss.* 2.20.10–15; Philo *Somn.* 1.117, 121, 164; 2.106, 133, 160, 162, 292; *Migr. Abr.* 222; *Odes Sol.* 8.3–5; *4 Macc.* 5:11; *Corp. herm.* 1.15.23; *Corp. herm.* 13.4; 1 Thessalonians 5:6–10; Mark 13:33–37; Ephesians 5:14; Matthew 24:43; Luke 12:39; Revelations 3:2–3; 16:15. Especially interesting is *Test. Reuben* 3:1–8, where sleep is figured as a destructive spirit within human nature: "Besides all these there is an eighth spirit of sleep (*pneuma tou hupnou*), with which is brought about the trance of nature (*ekstasis phuseōs*) and the image of death (*eikōn tou thanatou*). With these spirits are mingled the spirits of error.... And with all these the spirit of sleep is joined which is that of error and fantasy (*plane kai phantasia*)." For *ekstasis tēs phuseōs* as "degeneracy," see Theophrastus *CP* 3.1.6. Cf. Heinrich Balz, "*hupnos, ktl.*," *Theological*

Dictionary of the New Testament 8 (1972): 547–53; Heinrich Schlier, *Der Römerbrief*, Herders theologischer Kommentar zum Neuen Testament 6 (Freiburg: Herder, 1977), 396; James D. G. Dunn, *Romans 9–16*, Word Biblical Commentary 38b (Dallas: Word, 1988), 786; Robert Jewett, *Romans: A Commentary*, Hermeneia (Minneapolis: Fortress Press, 2007), 820.

2. On the gloominess of the vision of Silver Age writers, see, in general, D. Henry and E. Henry, *The Mask of Power: Seneca's Tragedies and Imperial Rome* (Warminster: Aris and Phillips, 1985); Thomas N. Habinek, *The Politics of Latin Literature: Writing, Identity, and Empire in Ancient Rome* (Princeton: Princeton University Press, 1998); John G. Fitch, *Seneca VIII Tragedies*, Loeb Classical Library 62 (Cambridge, Mass.: Harvard University Press, 2002), 5–10, 21–27; J. G. Fitch and S. McElduff, "Construction of the Self in Senecan Drama," *Mnemosyne* 55 (2002): 18–40; Paul Allen Miller, *Subjecting Verses: Latin Love Elegy and the Emergence of the Real* (Princeton: Princeton University Press, 2003), esp. 184–209; C. A. J. Littlewood, "The Broken World," in *Self-Representation and Illusion in Senecan Tragedy* (Oxford: Oxford University Press, 2004), 15–102; Basil Dufallo, *The Ghosts of the Past: Latin Literature, the Dead, and Rome's Transition to a Principate* (Columbus: Ohio State University Press, 2007).

3. In what follows, I choose Seneca as a particularly productive interlocutor for Paul because of Seneca's proximity and exposure to the forces unleashed by the structure of sole sovereignty. See, in general, Paul Veyne, *Seneca: The Life of a Stoic* (London: Routledge, 2003).

4. Seneca *Herc. Fur.* 610–11; unless otherwise indicated, translations are from Frank Justus Miller, *Seneca VIII Tragedies*, Loeb Classical Library 62 (Cambridge, MA: Harvard University Press, 1968), 57. See the commentary on this passage by Margarethe Billerbeck, *Seneca: "Hercules Furens": Einleitung, Text, Übersetzung und Kommentar* (Leiden: Brill, 1999), 411. On the function of tragedy in the political and cultural life of the first century, see Anthony J. Boyle, *Roman Tragedy* (London: Routledge, 2005).

5. Seneca *Herc. Fur.* 690. On the personification of Sleep (*Sopor*) here, see the commentary in John G. Fitch, *Seneca's "Hercules Furens": A Critical Text with Introduction and Commentary* (Ithaca: Cornell University Press, 1987), 300–301.

6. Seneca *Herc. Fur.* 704-705.
7. Ibid., 838, 849-53; see Fitch, *Seneca's "Hercules Furens,"* 337.
8. Seneca *Herc. Fur.* 843; see Fitch, *Seneca's "Hercules Furens,"* 339-40: "the singular (*somnos*) means 'the condition of sleep.'"
9. Seneca *Herc. Fur.* 861-63; trans. Fitch, *Seneca VIII Tragedies*, 117; see the commentary by Fitch, *Seneca's "Hercules Furens,"* 342, 343.
10. Seneca *Herc. Fur.* 1069; trans. Fitch, *Seneca VIII Tragedies*, 135; see the commentary in Fitch, *Seneca's "Hercules Furens,"* 397.
11. Seneca *Herc. Fur.* 1075-76; cf. Philo *Somn.* 2.667 M; Plutarch *Mor.* 107E; see the commentary in Fitch, *Seneca's "Hercules Furens,"* 398-99.
12. Seneca *Herc. Fur.* 137-38, 176-77; trans. Fitch, *Seneca VIII Tragedies*, 59, 61. 63; see the commentary by Billerbeck, *Seneca: "Hercules Furens,"* 262.
13. Seneca *Herc. Fur.* 860; trans. Fitch, *Seneca VIII Tragedies*, 117. See the discussion in James R. Harrison, "Paul and the 'Social Relations' of Death at Rome," in *Paul and His Social Relations*, ed. Stanley E. Porter and Christopher D. Land (Leiden: Brill, 2012), 101-5
14. Seneca *Oed.* 126-32; see the discussion in Billerbeck, *Seneca: "Hercules Furens,"* 483.
15. For example, Ovid *Tristia* 1.3; 3.2, 11; *Ex Ponto* 1.9; see the discussion of this phenomenon in Miller, *Subjecting Verses*, 210-36; Dufallo, *Ghosts of the Past*, 123-27.
16. Mark 14:28; Matthew 16:21; 26:32; Luke 9:22; see Jakob Kremer, "*egeirein*," *Exegetical Dictionary of the New Testament* 1 (1990): 372; Michael Thompson, *Clothed with Christ: The Example and Teaching of Jesus in Romans 12,1–15,13* (Sheffield: Sheffield Academic Press, 1991), 145: "*egeirein* (41x in the Pauline corpus) refers in every other case except Rom. 13:11 and Eph. 5: 14 to resurrection"; Jewett, *Romans*, 820.
17. Seneca *Herc. Fur.* 161, 163; see Fitch, *Seneca's "Hercules Furens,"* 174; Billerbeck, *Seneca: "Hercules Furens,"* 256-57.
18. Seneca *Herc. Fur.* 164-65; see Fitch, *Seneca's "Hercules Furens,"* 174.
19. Seneca *Herc. Fur.* 169-71; trans. Fitch, *Seneca VIII Tragedies*, 61; see Billerbeck, *Seneca: "Hercules Furens,"* 260-61.
20. Seneca *Herc. Fur.* 183-85; see *Seneca's "Hercules Furens,"* 177.

21. Keith Hopkins, *Death and Renewal: Sociological Studies in Roman History* (Cambridge: Cambridge University Press, 1983), 2:205–11; Timothy Peter Wiseman, *Catullus and His World* (Cambridge: Cambridge University Press, 1985), 4–14; Peter Garnsey and Richard Saller, *The Roman Empire: Economy, Society, and Culture* (London: Duckworth, 1987); Geza Alfölfy, *The Social History of Rome* (Baltimore: Johns Hopkins University Press, 1991), 135; Magnus Wistrand, *Entertainment and Violence in Ancient Rome: The Attitudes of Writers of the First Century* A.D. (Göteborg: Acta Universitatis Gothoburgensis, 1992); Roland Auguet, *Cruelty and Civilization: The Roman Games* (London: Routledge, 1994).

22. Rodolfo Lanciani, *Ancient Rome in the Light of Recent Archaeological Discoveries* (London: Macmillan, 1888), 64–67, summarized by Hopkins, *Death and Renewal*, 207–10. See now John Bodel, "Graveyards and Groves: A Study of the Lex Lucerina," *American Journal of Ancient History* 11 (1986): 1–133, esp. 40–47. Bodel (81–83, 114n194) suggests that mass crematoria replaced mass inhumation in the first century C.E., appealing to Martial 8.75.9–10 and Lucan 8.736–38.

23. Keith Hopkins, *Conquerors and Slaves: Sociological Studies in Roman History* (Cambridge: Cambridge University Press, 1978), 1:1–132; Keith Bradley, *Slavery and Society at Rome* (Cambridge: Cambridge University Press, 1994), esp. 166–67; Willem Jongman, "Slavery and the Growth of Rome: The Transformation of Italy in the Second and First Centuries BCE," in *Rome the Cosmopolis*, ed. Catherine Edwards and Greg Woolf (Cambridge: Cambridge University Press, 2003), 100–22.

24. Text of the inscription published in *L'année épigraphique* (1971): 88 and 89; English translation in Jane F. Gardner and Thomas Wiedemann, *The Roman Household: A Sourcebook* (London: Routledge, 1991), no. 22; see the discussion in O. F. Robinson, "Slaves and the Criminal Law," *Zeitschrift der Savigny-Stiftung für Rechtsgeschichte* 98 (1981): 223–27; Bradley, *Slavery and Society at Rome*, 166–67. On the crucifixion of slaves, see further Keith Bradley, *Slaves and Masters in the Roman Empire: A Study in Social Control* (Oxford: Oxford University Press, 1987), 113–37; Martin Hengel, *Crucifixion in the Ancient World and the Folly of the Message of the Cross* (Philadelphia: Fortress Press, 1977), 33–51.

25. Hopkins, *Death and Renewal*, 11, 12, 29; Miller, *Subjecting Verses*, 184–209. On the Principate as a "state of exception" in the Schmittian sense, see Giorgio Agamben, *State of Exception*, trans. Kevin Attell (Chicago: University of Chicago Press, 2005), 65–88.
26. For example, Tacitus *Ann.* 1.2.1; 4.1 on the slavishness fostered by Augustus and his successors and the destruction of the Roman character. Cf. Hopkins, *Death and Renewal*, 3, 10; Miller, *Subjecting Verses*, 210–36; Dufallo, *Ghosts of the Past*, 123–27.
27. Seneca *Herc. Fur.* 64–65.
28. Ibid., 67–68.
29. Fitch, *Seneca's "Hercules Furens,"* 34–35; 39–40; cf. A. Rose, "Seneca's *HF*: A Politic-Didactic Reading," *CJ* 75 (1979–80): 135–42, esp. 141; G. Bruden, "Herakles and Hercules: Survival in Greek and Roman Tragedy," in *Theater and Society in the Classical World*, ed. R. Scodel (Ann Arbor: University of Michigan Press, 1993), 251. See, in general, Anthony A. Barrett, *Caligula: The Corruption of Power* (New Haven: Yale University Press, 1990), 213–41; Aloys Winterling, *Caligula: A Biography* (Berkeley: University of California Press, 2011), 132–71.
30. Philo *Leg. Gai.* 75.
31. Suetonius *Gaius Caligula*, esp. 32–36; see also Philo *Leg. Gai.* 66, 89–90, 101.
32. Cassius Dio 59.10; cf. Hopkins, *Death and Renewal*, 10. One should acknowledge that Cassius Dio is characterizing the reign of Caligula long after the fact. But abject fear is already attested by Epictetus *Diss.* 1.1.26; 1.3.2, and so on in passages enjoining his hearers not to be afraid that Caesar is going to kill you—are you the only one with a neck to be bared to the executioner?
33. Hopkins, *Death and Renewal*, 11, 29.
34. P. A. Brunt and J. M. Moore, *Res gestae divi Augusti* (Oxford: Oxford University Press, 1967), 22, 25.
35. Cassius Dio 49.12.
36. Suetonius *Claud.* 34. See further Catherine Edwards, "Death as Spectacle: Looking at Death in the Arena," in *Death in Ancient Rome* (New Haven: Yale University Press, 2007), 46–77.

37. Harold N. Fowler and Richard Stillwell, *Corinth* (Cambridge, Mass.: Harvard University Press, 1932), 1:1:89–91, 79 (figs. 54–56, with plan); Ferdinand J. de Waele, *Theater en Amphitheater Te Oud Korinthe* (Utrecht: Dekker, 1928), 25–31; Katherine Welch, "Negotiating Roman Spectacle Architecture in the Greek World: Athens and Corinth," in *The Art of Ancient Spectacle*, ed. Bettina Bergmann and Christine Kondoleon (New Haven: Yale University Press, 1999), 125–45, esp. 133–40.
38. Louis Robert, *Les gladiateurs dans l'Orient grec* (Paris: Champion, 1940), 270; Hopkins, *Death and Renewal*, 13.
39. On the psychological lure of spectacle, see Paul Veyne, *Le pain et le cirque: Sociologie historique d'un pluralisme politique* (Paris: Seuil, 1976); Hopkins, *Death and Renewal*, 2–3, 7–12, 17, 26; Carlin A. Barton, *The Sorrows of the Ancient Romans: The Gladiator and the Monster* (Princeton: Princeton University Press, 1993), esp. 47–106; Richard Beacham, *Spectacle Entertainments of Early Imperial Rome* (New Haven: Yale University Press, 1999), 128, 240; Garratt G. Fagan, *The Lure of the Arena: Social Psychology and the Crowd at the Roman Games* (Cambridge: Cambridge University Press, 2011).
40. Seneca *Herc. Fur.* 838–39; see Fitch, *Seneca's "Hercules Furens,"* 338.
41. Tacitus *Dial. Or.* 29.
42. Seneca *Ep. Mor.* 7.5. Of course, one should recognize that Seneca and Tacitus may impute to the masses desires and motivations that may not have been their own. For an attempt to gain access to the mental world of the lower classes, see Nicholas Horsfall, *The Culture of the Roman Plebs* (London: Bloomsbury Academic, 2003).
43. Tertullian *De Spect.* 12, 21.
44. Seneca *Ep. Mor.* 7.3.
45. Ibid., 7.5.
46. Ranuccio Bianchi Bandinelli, Mario Torelli, Filippo Coarelli, and Antonio Giuliano, "Il monument teatino di C. Lusius Storax nel Museo di Chieti," *Studi Miscellanei* 10, no. 3 (1963–64): 55–102. See the analysis and interpretation of this monument in John R. Clarke, *Art in the Lives of Ordinary Romans: Visual Representation and Non-Elite Viewers in Italy, 100 B.C.–A.D. 315* (Berkeley: University of California Press, 2003), 145–52, esp. 151–52.

47. G. De Petra, "L'anfiteatro pompeiano rappresentato in un antico dipinto," *Giornale degli scavi di Pompei* 1 (1868–69): 185–86; more recently, Valeria Sampaolo, "I 3, 23: Casa della Rissa nel-l'Anfiteatro," in *Pompei: Pitture e mosaic* 1 (Rome: Instituto della Enciclopedia Italiana, 1990), 77–81. See the analysis and discussion in Clark, *Art in the Lives of Ordinary Romans*, 152–58. It has long been recognized by scholars that the painting is an illustration of the riot described by Tacitus in *Ann.* 14.17.
48. See the parallel texts adduced by C. E. B. Cranfield, *A Critical and Exegetical Commentary on the Epistle to the Romans*, ICC (Edinburgh: T and T Clark, 1979), 2:687–88; Schlier, *Der Römerbrief,* 398–99; Thompson, *Clothed with Christ,* 149; Dunn, *Romans 9–16,* 789–90; Jewett, *Romans,* 825–27; especially interesting is the account of Nero's nocturnal behavior in Suetonius *Nero* 26: "No sooner was the twilight over than he would catch up a cap or a wig and go to the taverns or range about the streets playing pranks, which however were very far from harmless; for he used to beat men as they came home from dinner, stabbing any who resisted and throwing them into the sewers.... In the strife which resulted he often ran the risk of losing his eyes or even his life, for he was beaten almost to death by a man of the senatorial order, whose wife he had maltreated."
49. Bruce Winter, "Roman Law and Society in Romans 12–15," in *Rome in the Bible and the Early Church*, ed. Peter Oakes (Grand Rapids, Mich.: Baker Books, 2002), 67–102, here 86–88; Jewett, *Romans*, 824–27.
50. Giuseppe Fiorelli, "Pompei," *Notizie degli scavi di antichità* 1 (1876): 193–95; August Mau, "Scavi di Pompei," *Bullettino dell'Instituto di Corrispondenza Archeologica* (1878): 191–94; Irene Bragantini, "VI 14, 35.36: Caupona di Salvius," in *Pompei: Pitture e mosaic* 5 (Rome: Instituto della Enciclopedia Italiana, 1994), 366–71. For analysis and interpretation, see Clarke, *Art in the Lives of Ordinary Romans*, 161–68.
51. For the text of the captions, see Mau, "Scavi di Pompei," 194. On the relationship between the captions and the images, see Clarke, *Art in the Lives of Ordinary Romans*, 161.
52. Mau, "Scavi di Pompei," 194; cf. F. A. Todd, "Three Pompeian Wall-Inscriptions, and Petronius," *Classical Review* 53 (1939): 5–8, here 6; Clarke, *Art in the Lives of Ordinary Romans*, 165.

53. Mau, "Scavi di Pompei," 194; see Clarke, *Art in the Lives of Ordinary Romans*, 162–64.
54. Mau, "Scavi di Pompei," 194; cf. Todd, "Three Pompeian Wall-Inscriptions," 8; Clarke, *Art in the Lives of Ordinary Romans*, 167.
55. Cranfield, *Epistle to the Romans*, 2:687: "The relation between the two nouns in each pair is very close: each pair may, in fact, be understood as suggesting one composite idea (e.g. drunken revelries) rather than two distinct ideas"; see, similarly, Dunn, *Romans 9–16*, 789.
56. Clarke, *Art in the Lives of Ordinary Romans*, 161, 162, 167–68.
57. Reading *apobalōmetha* (let us cast off) in 13:12b (reasonably well attested by P46, D*, F, G), rather than *apothōmetha* (let us put off), with C. E. B. Cranfield, *A Commentary on Romans 12–13*, vol. 12, *Occasional Papers of the Scottish Journal of Theology* (Edinburgh: Oliver and Boyd, 1965), 94; similarly, Jewett, *Romans*, 816, 822, who comments: "This wording carries forward the idea of rising from sleep and casting off bed covering."
58. Seneca *Herc. Fur.* 1044–46; see Fitch, *Seneca's "Hercules Furens*,*"* 388–89.
59. Seneca *Herc. Fur.* 1051–52; see Fitch, *Seneca's "Hercules Furens*,*"* 390.
60. Rose, "Seneca's HF: A Politic-Didactic Reading," 135–42; Fitch, *Seneca's "Hercules Furens*,*"* 34–35, 39–40.
61. Seneca *Herc. Fur.* 1065–81; see the discussion of addresses and prayers to Sleep in Fitch, *Seneca's "Hercules Furens*,*"* 394–95.
62. Seneca *Herc. Fur.* 1083; trans. Fitch, *Seneca VIII Tragedies*, 137; see the commentary in Fitch, *Seneca's "Hercules Furens*,*"* 400–401.

4. AWAKENING (C′)

1. Ps-Plato *Cleitophon* 407B–408C; Epictetus *Diss.* 2.20.10–15; Philo *Somn.* 1.164; 2.292; *Odes Sol.* 8:3–5; Ephesians 5:14; *Corp. herm.* 1.15.23, 27; *Corp. herm.* 7.1; *Corp. herm.* 13.4; *Acts Thom.* 110.43–44. Cf. Evald Lövestam, *Spiritual Wakefulness in the New Testament* (Lund: Gleerup, 1963), 26; Heinrich Schlier, *Der Römerbrief*, Herders theologischer Kommentar zum Neuen Testament 6 (Freiburg: Herder, 1977), 396; Robert Jewett, *Romans: A Commentary*, Hermeneia (Minneapolis: Fortress Press, 2007), 820.
2. Ps.-Plato *Cleitophon* 408C; see Simon Roelof Slings, *A Commentary on the Platonic Clitophon* (Amsterdam: Academische Pers, 1981), 118, 329,

who suggests that the author was thinking of the famous comparison of Socrates with a gadfly in Plato *Apol.* 30E2–5 and 31A4.

3. Epictetus *Diss.* 2.20.10; cited in Jewett, *Romans*, 820.
4. Epictetus *Diss.* 2.20.15–16. Cf. A. A. Long, *Epictetus: A Stoic and Socratic Guide to Life* (Oxford: Oxford University Press, 2002), 186.
5. *Corp. herm.* 1.27; see Richard Reitzenstein, *Poimandres: Studien zur griechisch-ägyptischen und frühchristlichen Literatur* (Leipzig: Teubner, 1904), 58–59; George MacRae, "Sleep and Awakening in Gnostic Texts," in *The Origins of Gnosticism*, ed. U. Bianchi (Leiden: Brill, 1967), 504. See, in general, Ernst Haenchen, "Aufbau und Theologie des *Poimandres*," in *Gott und Mensch* (Tübingen: Mohr, 1965), 335–77. C. H. Dodd dates the *Poimandres* between 130 and 140 C.E. Dodd, *The Bible and the Greeks* (London: Hodder and Stoughton, 1935), 209.
6. Lövestam, *Spiritual Wakefulness*, 26; Schlier, *Der Römerbrief*, 396; Jewett, *Romans*, 820.
7. Ps.-Plato *Cleitophon* 408B; see Slings, *A Commentary on the Platonic Clitophon*, 338: "This is of course the central motif of all Socratic protreptic."
8. Ps.-Plato *Cleitophon* 408A; see Slings, *A Commentary on the Platonic Clitophon*, 334.
9. Epictetus *Diss.* 2.20.15.
10. Ibid., 2.20.17–18.
11. Ibid., 2.20.13.
12. *Corp. herm.* 1.1–2; text cited according to the edition of A. D. Nock and A.-J. Festugière, *Corpus Hermeticum*, vol. 1, *Traités I–XII* (Paris: Société d'édition "Les belle lettres," 1945).
13. *Corp. herm.* 1.3.
14. Ibid., 1.8.
15. Ibid., 1.21; see Hans Dieter Betz, "The Delphic Maxim GNŌTHI SAUTON in Hermetic Interpretation," in *Hellenismus und Urchristentum: Gesammelte Aufsätze I* (Tübingen: Mohr Siebeck, 1990), 92–111, esp. 94–95.
16. *Corp. herm.* 1.30. Cf. P. J. Södergard, *The Hermetic Piety of the Mind: A Semiotic and Cognitive Study of the Discourse of Hermes Trismegistos* (Stockholm: Almqvist and Wiksell, 2003).

17. On the possibility of development in Paul's eschatology, see Albert Schweitzer, *The Mysticism of Paul the Apostle*, trans. William Montgomery (Baltimore: Johns Hopkins University Press, 1998), 91–100; C. H. Dodd, "The Mind of Paul, II," in *New Testament Studies* (Manchester: Manchester University Press, 1953), 108–28; Günther Klein, "Apokalyptische Naherwartung bei Paulus," in *Neues Testament und christliche Existenz*, ed. H. D. Betz and L. Schottroff (Tübingen: Mohr Siebeck, 1973), 241–62; Gerd Lüdemann, *Paulus, der Heiden Apostel*, vol. 1, *Studien zur Chronologie* (Göttingen: Vandenhoeck und Ruprecht, 1980), 213–70.

18. With the majority of critical scholars, I do not regard 2 Thessalonians, Colossians, or Ephesians as authentically Pauline: see William Wrede, *Die Echtheit des II. Thessalonicherbriefes* (Leipzig: Hinrichs, 1902); Herbert Braun, "Zur nichtpaulinischen Herkunft des zweiten Thessalonicherbriefes," in *Studien zum Neuen Testament und seiner Umwelt* (Tübingen: Mohr Siebeck, 1971), 205–9; Wolfgang Trilling, *Untersuchungen zum zweiten Thessalonicherbrief* (Leipzig: St. Benno-Verlag, 1972); Edgar Krentz, "A Stone That Will Not Fit: The Non-Pauline Authorship of Second Thessalonians," in *Pseudepigraphie und Verfasserfiktion in frühchristlichen Briefen*, ed. Jörg Frey et al. (Tübingen: Mohr Siebeck, 2009), 433–38; Eduard Lohse, *Colossians and Philemon: A Commentary on the Epistles to Colossians and Philemon*, Hermeneia (Philadelphia: Fortress Press, 1971); Helmut Koester, *Introduction to the New Testament*, vol. 2, *History and Literature of Early Christianity*, 2nd ed. (Berlin: de Gruyter, 2000), 247–50, 266–72.

19. For the translation, compare Hans Dieter Betz, *Galatians: A Commentary on Paul's Letter to the Churches in Galatia*, Hermeneia (Philadelphia: Fortress Press, 1979), 57. As is well known, there are no explicit references to the *parousia* in Galatians. For the debate on the eschatology of Galatians, see J. Christiaan Beker, *Paul the Apostle: The Triumph of God in Life and Thought* (Philadelphia: Fortress Press, 1980), 37–58; J. Louis Martyn, "Apocalyptic Antinomies in the Letter to the Galatians," *New Testament Studies* 31 (1985): 307–24; Martyn, *Galatians: A New Translation with Introduction and Commentary*, Anchor Bible 33A (New York: Doubleday, 1985), passim; M. C. de Boer, "Paul and Apocalyptic Eschatology," in *The*

Continuum History of Apocalypticism, ed. Bernard McGinn, John J. Collins, and Stephen J. Stein (New York: Continuum, 2003), 183.
20. Betz, *Galatians*, 70–71; de Boer, "Paul and Apocalyptic Eschatology," 174.
21. John Knox, *Chapters in a Life of Paul*, rev. ed. (Macon: Mercer University Press, 1987), 95–99; Günther Bornkamm, *Paul* (New York: Harper and Row, 1971), 17–21.
22. 1 Corinthians 9:1, *ouchi Iēsoun ton kurion hēmōn heoraka* (Have I not seen Jesus our Lord?); 1 Corinthians 15:8, *ōphthē kamoi* (he [sc. the Messiah] appeared also to me). The distinction between Paul's use of *horan* (to see) in 1 Corinthians 9:1; 15:8 and *apokaluptein* (to reveal) in Galatians 1:16 has been pointed out by a number of scholars: Alfred Wikenhauser, *Die Christusmystik des Apostels Paulus* (Freiburg: Herder, 1956), 88–90; Hans Lietzmann, *An die Galater*, Handbuch zum Neuen Testament 10 (Tübingen: Mohr Siebeck, 1971), 7–8; Heinrich Schlier, *Der Brief an die Galater*, Kritisch-exegetischer Kommentar über das Neue Testament 7 (Göttingen: Vandenhoeck und Ruprecht, 1971), 55; Betz, *Galatians*, 71; de Boer, "Paul and Apocalyptic Eschatology," 174.
23. Walter Bauer, *A Greek-English Lexicon of the New Testament and Other Early Christian Literature*, 3rd ed., rev. and ed. Frederick William Danker (Chicago: University of Chicago Press, 2000), 112, s.v., *apokaluptō*; 201, s.v., *apokaluptō*; cf. Albrecht Oepke, "*apokaluptō ktl.*," *Theological Dictionary of the New Testament* 3 (1965): 563–92, with the caveat on 564: "Unusual difficulties of method confront this lexical investigation. Because of ecclesiastical dogmatics, an unclarified pre-understanding of the subject is often imported into the normal translations 'to reveal' and 'revelation.'" Especially interesting in connection with Galatians 1:16 is *Corp. herm.* 13:1: *ainigmatōdōs kai ou tēlaugōs ephrasas peri theiotētos dialegomenos; ouk apekalupsas, phamenos mēdena dunasthai sōthēnai pro tēs paliggenesias* (Enigmatically and not clearly you spoke when discussing divinity; you did not reveal it since, as you said, no one is able to be saved before regeneration); see William C. Grese, *Corpus Hermeticum XIII and Early Christian Literature* (Leiden: Brill, 1979), 3–4, 62.
24. F. Blass and A. Debrunner, *A Greek Grammar of the New Testament and Other Early Christian Literature*, trans. and rev. R. W. Funk (Chicago:

University of Chicago Press, 1961), §220.1; Bauer, *A Greek-English Lexicon*, 329, s.v., *en* 8; Dieter Lührmann, *Das Offenbarungsverständnis bei Paulus und in paulinischen Gemeinden* (Neukirchen-Vluyn: Neukirchener Verlag, 1965), 79n1; Franz Mussner, *Der Galaterbrief*, Herders theologischer Kommentar zum Neuen Testament 9 (Freiburg: Herder, 1974), 86-87.

25. Betz, *Galatians*, 71: "There are indications that we should take his [Paul's] words [*en emoi*] seriously. The 'in me' corresponds to Gal. 2:20 ('Christ... lives in me').... This would mean that Paul's experience was ecstatic in nature."

26. In an earlier era, Paul's experience as reported in Galatians 1:16 was interpreted as "mystical": see Richard Reitzenstein, *Die hellenistischen Mysterienreligionen nach ihren Grundgedanken und Wirkungen*, 3rd ed. (Stuttgart: Teubner, 1927), 371; Schweitzer, *The Mysticism of Paul the Apostle*, 90-100, 181, and passim; Béda Rigaux, *Letters of Saint Paul*, ed. and trans. Stephen Yonick (Chicago: Franciscan Herald, 1968), 51-55. More recently, this view has been revived on the basis of analysis of Jewish mystical texts by Alan Segal, *Paul the Convert: The Apostolate and Apostasy of Saul the Pharisee* (New Haven: Yale University Press, 1990), 20-21, 39-52.

27. Galatians 1:1, 4, 11; 3:13; 4:4-6; see Betz, *Galatians*, 70-71; de Boer, "Paul and Apocalyptic Eschatology," 173-75.

28. Wolfgang Schrage, "Der gekreuzigte und auferweckte Herr," *Zeitschrift für Theologie und Kirche* 94 (1997): 25-38, esp. 25-26; Theo K. Heckel, "Der Gekreuzigte bei Paulus und im Markusevangelium," *Biblische Zeitschrift* 46 (2002): 190-210, esp. 194-95; Heinz-Wolfgang Kuhn, "Kreuz," *Theologische Realenzyklopädie* 19 (1990): 720.

29. L. L. Welborn, *Paul, the Fool of Christ: A Study of 1 Corinthians 1-4 in the Comic-Philosophic Tradition* (London: T and T Clark, 2005), 234; Welborn, "The Culture of Crucifixion and the Resurrection of the Dispossessed," in *Paul and the Philosophers*, ed. Ward Blanton and Hent de Vries (New York: Fordham University Press, 2013); Stanislas Breton, *The Word and the Cross*, trans. Jacquelyn Porter (New York: Fordham University Press, 2002).

30. Dieter Georgi, *Theocracy in Paul's Praxis and Theology* (Minneapolis: Fortress Press, 1991), 54; Alain Badiou, *Saint Paul: The Foundation of Universalism*, trans. Ray Brassier (Stanford: Stanford University Press, 2003),

46–47; Justin Meggitt, *Paul, Poverty and Survival* (Edinburgh: T and T Clark, 1998), 75–76, 96–100; Welborn, *Paul, the Fool of Christ*, 2, 7, 147, 164, 233–34.

31. Hans Windisch, *Der zweite Korintherbrief*, Kritisch-exegetischer Kommentar über das Neue Testament (1924; Göttingen: Vandenhoeck und Ruprecht, 1970), 181–82; Erich Dinkler, "Die Verkündigung als eschatologisch-sakramentales Geschehen: Auslegung von 2 Kor 5,14– 6,2," in *Die Zeit Jesu*, ed. Günther Bornkamm and Karl Rahner (Freiburg: Herder, 1970), 169–89, esp. 186–87; Rudolf Bultmann, *Der zweite Brief an die Korinther*, Kritisch-exegetischer Kommentar über das Neue Testament (Göttingen: Vandenhoeck und Ruprecht, 1976), 151–53; Victor Paul Furnish, *II Corinthians*, Anchor Bible 32A (Garden City, N.Y.: Doubleday, 1984), 310, 326–28; Cilliers Breytenbach, "'Christus starb für uns': Zur Tradition und paulinischen Rezeption des sogenannten 'Sterbeformeln,'" *New Testament Studies* 29 (2003): 447–75.

32. Windisch, *Der zweite Korintherbrief*, 181; Bultmann, *Der zweite Brief*, 152– 53; Furnish, *II Corinthians*, 309–10.

33. Reitzenstein, *Die hellenistischen Mysterienreligionen*, 372–73; Windisch, *Der zweite Korintherbrief*, 182; Robert C. Tannehill, *Dying and Rising with Christ: A Study in Pauline Theology* (Berlin: Töpelmann, 1967), 66; Furnish, *II Corinthians*, 327.

34. Betz, *Galatians*, 121–22, calling attention to the similarity of Paul's first-person singular style to the synthemata of the mystery cults collected in Albrecht Dieterich, *Eine Mithrasliturgie* (Darmstadt: Wissenschaftliche Buchgesellschaft, 1966), 213–19. See already Reitzenstein, *Die hellenistischen Mysterienreligionen*, 260–61.

35. Tannehill, *Dying and Rising with Christ*, 22, 42; Hubert Frankemölle, *Das Taufverständnis bei Paulus: Taufe, Tod und Auferstehung nach Röm 6* (Stuttgart: Katholisches Bibelwerk, 1970), 41–53; Alexander J. M. Wedderburn, *Baptism and Resurrection: Studies in Pauline Theology Against Its Graeco-Roman Background* (Tübingen: Mohr Siebeck, 1987), 46–49; Hans Dieter Betz, "Transferring a Ritual: Paul's Interpretation of Baptism in Romans 6," in *Paulinische Studien: Gesammelte Aufsätze 3* (Tübingen: Mohr Siebeck, 1994), 240–71, esp. 261–70.

36. Windisch, *Der zweite Korintherbrief*, 144–47; Tannehill, *Dying and Rising with Christ*, 85–86; Bultmann, *Der zweite Brief*, 117–22; Furnish, *II Corinthians*, 255–56, 283–84; Timothy Luckritz Marquis, *Transient Apostle: Paul, Travel, and the Rhetoric of Empire*, Synkrisis (New Haven: Yale University Press, 2013), 112–14.
37. *Pss. Sol.* 17:23–35; 18:5–7; cf. Robert B. Wright, "Psalms of Solomon," in *The Old Testament Pseudepigrapha*, ed. James H. Charlesworth (Garden City, N.Y.: Doubleday, 1985), 2:643–46; Andrew Chester, *Messiah and Exaltation: Jewish Messianic and Visionary Traditions and New Testament Christology* (Tübingen: Mohr Siebeck, 2007), 342–43.
38. Paul Veyne, *Seneca: The Life of a Stoic* (London: Routledge, 2003), 167; James Ker, *The Deaths of Seneca* (Oxford: Oxford University Press, 2009), 17–40, 41–64.
39. Seneca *Ep. Mor.* 70; cf. Ker, *Deaths of Seneca*, 147–76.
40. Seneca *Ep. Mor.* 77. See also *Ep. Mor.* 61 and the panegyric of death in *Ad Marciam* 20. Cf. Ker, *Deaths of Seneca*, 147–76.
41. See the account of Seneca's death in Tacitus *Ann.* 15.62–64; cf. Ker, *Deaths of Seneca*, 17–40.
42. Seneca *Herc. Fur.* 1258–62; cf. John G. Fitch, *Seneca's "Hercules Furens": A Critical Text with Introduction and Commentary* (Ithaca: Cornell University Press, 1987), 439–40.
43. For Seneca, see the essays collected in Shadi Bartsch and David Wray, eds., *Seneca and the Self* (Cambridge: Cambridge University Press, 2009), esp. Austin Busch, "Dissolution of the Self in the Senecan Corpus," 255–82.
44. For the concept of a messianic "partition" of the self in the thought of Paul, see Giorgio Agamben, *The Time That Remains: A Commentary on the Letter to the Romans*, trans. Patricia Daley (Stanford: Stanford University Press, 2005), 49–53. See already, in somewhat different terms, Reitzenstein, *Die hellenistischen Mysterienreligionen*, 260–61; Schweitzer, *The Mysticism of Paul the Apostle*, 3, 119, 121, 125.
45. Schweitzer, *The Mysticism of Paul the Apostle*, 222; Windisch, *Der zweite Korintherbrief*, 183–84; Dinkler, "Auslegung von 2 Kor 5,14–6,2," 172; Furnish, *II Corinthians*, 311. See further John Ashton, *The Religion of Paul the Apostle* (Suffolk: St. Edmundsbury Press, 2000).

46. Reitzenstein, *Die hellenistischen Mysterienreligionen*, 349, 371–73; Rigaux, *Letters of Saint Paul*, 51–55; Betz, *Galatians*, 71.

47. For the interpretation of the expression *pistis Iēsou Christou* as "the faith (or faithfulness) of Messiah Jesus," see Richard Hays, *The Faith of Jesus Christ: The Narrative Substructure of Galatians 3:1–4:11*, 2nd ed. (Grand Rapids, Mich.: Eerdmans, 2002).

48. Plato *Phaedr.* 66E–67A; see also Philo *Gig.* 14; cf. Bultmann, *Der zweite Brief*, 120.

49. Bultmann, *Der zweite Brief*, 121–22.

5. KAIROS (B')

1. See later in this chapter for a comparison of Romans 13:11–14 with 1 Thessalonians 5:2–10.

2. 2 *Apoc. Bar.* 23:7; Mark 13:28–29; see the discussion in A. L. Moore, *The Parousia in the New Testament* (Leiden: Brill, 1966), 122; C. E. B. Cranfield, *A Critical and Exegetical Commentary on the Epistle to the Romans*, ICC (Edinburgh: T and T Clark, 1979), 2:682–84; James D. G. Dunn, *Romans 9–16*, Word Biblical Commentary 38b (Dallas: Word, 1988), 786–87; Michael Thompson, *Clothed with Christ: The Example and Teaching of Jesus in Romans 12,1–15,13* (Sheffield: Sheffield Academic Press, 1991), 146–47; Robert Jewett, *Romans: A Commentary*, Hermeneia (Minneapolis: Fortress Press, 2007), 821.

3. For the tradition upon which Paul is drawing, see esp. Isaiah 59:17. Cf. Cranfield, *Epistle to the Romans*, 2:686: "*ta hopla* must mean 'armour,' and will include both defensive and offensive armour"; Otto Michel, *Der Brief an die Römer*, KEK 4 (Göttingen: Vandenhoeck und Ruprecht, 1978), 415; Ulrich Wilckens, *Der Brief an die Römer, 3. Teilband Röm 12–16*, Evangelisch-katholischer Kommentar (Zürich: Benziger Verlag, 1982), 77; Jewett, *Romans*, 822–23, citing Herodotus 7.218 on "men dressed in armor" (*enduomenous hopla*) and Xenophon *Cyr.* 1.4.18 describing Cyrus "then stepping into his armor for the first time" (*autos proton tote hoopla endus*).

4. Hans Conzelmann, "*phōs, ktl.*," *Theological Dictionary of the New Testament* 9 (1974): 312; Karl Georg Kuhn, "*hopla. ktl.*," *Theological Dictionary of the New Testament* 5 (1967): 298–300; Michel, *Der Römerbrief*, 415; Dunn,

Romans 9–16, 788, citing 1 Enoch 10:5; 92:4–5; 108:11–15; 2 Enoch 65:9–10; 2 Apoc. Bar. 18:2; 48:50; 1QS 1:9–10; 3:24–25; 4:7–13; 1QM 1:1, 8–14; 13:5–16.

5. 1 QM 13:14–16; text in *Die Texte aus Qumran*, ed. Eduard Lohse (München: Kösel Verlag, 1971), 210; translated into English as *The Dead Sea Scrolls in English*, trans. Geza Vermes (New York: Penguin, 1975), 141. Cf. Herbert Braun, *Qumran und das Neue Testament* (Tübingen: Mohr Siebeck, 1966), 1:222–24; Jewett, *Romans*, 824.

6. Edgar Haulotte, *Symbolique du vêtement selon la Bible* (Paris: Aubier, 1966), 212–13; Jewett, *Romans*, 823.

7. *humas* is chosen in Bruce Metzger, *A Textual Commentary on the Greek New Testament* (New York: United Bible Societies, 1975), 467; Cranfield, *Epistle to the Romans*, 2:680; Dunn, *Romans 9–16*, 784. Jewett, *Romans*, 816, argues for *hēmas* on rhetorical grounds.

8. Cranfield, *Epistle to the Romans*, 2:685; Jewett, *Romans*, 822.

9. Cranfield, *Epistle to the Romans*, 2:687; Schlier, *Der Römerbrief*, 398; Michel, *Der Brief an die Römer*, 416; Dunn, *Romans 9–16*, 789; Jewett, *Romans*, 825. For *euschēmonōs*, compare 1 Thessalonians 4:12; 1 Corinthians 14:40.

10. F. Blass and A. Debrunner, *A Greek Grammar of the New Testament and Other Early Christian Literature*, trans. and rev. R. W. Funk (Chicago: University of Chicago Press, 1961), §337; Jewett, *Romans*, 825.

11. Evald Lövestam, *Spiritual Wakefulness in the New Testament* (Lund: Gleerup, 1963), 41–45; Jewett, *Romans*, 827. The concept of "putting on" a redeemer figure has its background in the mystery religions: see Richard Reitzenstein, *Die hellenistischen Mysterienreligionen nach ihren Grundgedanken und Wirkungen*, 3rd ed. (Stuttgart: Teubner, 1927), 42–42, 60–62, 266, 350–51. On *endusasthe*, compare Galatians 3:27, with the comments of Betz, *Galatians*, 188.

12. J. H. Moulton and G. Milligan, *The Vocabulary of the Greek Testament Illustrated from the Papyri and Other Non-Literary Sources* (1930; Grand Rapids, Mich.: Eerdmans, 1985), 543, s.v., *pronoia*; cf. Michel, *Der Brief an die Römer*, 417n24; Jewett, *Romans*, 828.

13. In the history of scholarship, Paul's eschatology is usually derived from 1 Thessalonians and 1 Corinthians 15; see M. C. de Boer, "Paul and Apoc-

alyptic Eschatology," in *The Continuum History of Apocalypticism*, ed. Bernard McGinn, John J. Collins, and Stephen J. Stein (New York: Continuum, 2003), 166–67. Some scholars perceive a waning of interest in the *parousia* from the early to the late letters, for example, J. Christiaan Beker, *The Triumph of God: The Essence of Paul's Thought*, trans. L. Stuckenbruck (Minneapolis: Fortress Press, 1990), 31. Yet, Alexandra Brown probably voices the consensus (post Käsemann and Martyn) in saying: "But the letters taken together and read with attention to Paul's pervasive apocalyptic perspective demonstrate that the parousia hope, whether imminent or distant, is fundamental to his theological vision, ... even when it is not explicitly narrated." Brown, "Paul and the Parousia," in *The Return of Jesus in Early Christianity*, ed. John T. Carroll (Peabody: Hendrickson, 2000), 47–76, here 50–51. Cf. Ernst Käsemann, "On the Subject of Primitive Christian Apocalyptic," in *New Testament Questions of Today* (Philadelphia: Fortress Press, 1969), 108–37; Paul Hoffmann, *Die Toten in Christus: Eine religionsgeschichtliche und exegetische Untersuchung zur paulinischen Eschatologie* (Münster: Aschendorff, 1966); Joost Holleman, *Resurrection and Parousia: A Traditio-Historical Study of Paul's Eschatology in 1 Corinthians* (Leiden: Brill, 1996); Joseph Plevnik, *Paul and the Parousia: An Exegetical and Theological Investigation* (Peabody: Hendrickson, 1997).

14. Lövestam, *Spiritual Wakefulness*, 34–35; Michel, *Der Brief an die Römer*, 416; Thompson, *Clothed with Christ*, 145, 149; Jewett, *Romans*, 821.
15. Abraham J. Malherbe, *The Letters to the Thessalonians: A New Translation with Introduction and Commentary*, Anchor Bible 32B (New York: Doubleday, 2000), 295.
16. Lövestam, *Spiritual Wakefulness*, 34–35.
17. Walter Bauer, *A Greek-English Lexicon of the New Testament and Other Early Christian Literature*, 3rd ed., rev. and ed. Frederick William Danker (Chicago: University of Chicago Press, 2000), 852, s.v., *katheudō*; 490, s.v., *katheudō*. Cf. Malherbe, *Thessalonians*, 295.
18. Bauer, *A Greek-English Lexicon*, 1873, s.v., *hupnos*; Heinrich Balz, "*hupnos, ktl.*," *Theological Dictionary of the New Testament* 8 (1972): 547–48.
19. Lövestam, *Spiritual Wakefulness*, 35–37, 40–41; Dunn, *Romans 9–16*, 786. On sleep as a gnostic metaphor expressing "man's total abandonment to

the world," see Hans Jonas, *The Gnostic Religion: The Message of the Alien God and the Beginnings of Christianity* (Boston: Beacon, 2001), 70.

20. Hesiod *Th.* 212.
21. Homer *Il.* 14.231; 16.672, 682.
22. Bauer, *A Greek-English*, 360, s.v., *grēgoreō*; 207-8, s.v., *grēgoreō*. Cf. Lövestam, *Spiritual Wakefulness*, 45-58; Malherbe, *Thessalonians*, 295.
23. Bauer, *A Greek-English Lexicon*, 360, s.v., *grēgorēsis*; see Daniel 5:11 (Septuagint).
24. Bauer, *A Greek-English Lexicon*, 469, s.v., *egeirō* I.1, II.1; 271, s.v., *egeirō* 2; cf. Jewett, *Romans*, 820.
25. Cf. Philo *Somn.* 2.160-62.
26. Cf. Plutarch *Mor.* 781D, 800B.
27. Jakob Kremer, "*egeirō*," *Exegetical Dictionary of the New Testament* 1 (1990): 372.
28. Cf. *Test. Levi* 19:1; *Test. Benj.* 5:3; 1QM 15:9; see the discussion in Hans Conzelmann, "*skotos, ktl.*," *Theological Dictionary of the New Testament* 7 (1971): 442; Roman Heiligenthal, *Werke als Zeichen: Untersuchungen zur Bedeutung der menschlichen Taten im Frühjudentum, Neuen Testament und Frühchristentum* (Tübingen: Mohr Siebeck, 1983), 225-27; Malherbe, *Thessalonians*, 293-94.
29. Lövestam, *Spiritual Wakefulness*, 33; Vögtle, "Röm 13:11-14 und die 'Nah'-Erwartung," 566; Jewett, *Romans*, 821.
30. Gustav Stählin, "*prokoptō, ktl.*," *Theological Dictionary of the New Testament* 6 (1968): 716n85; Wolfgang Schrenk, "*prokoptō, prokopē*," *Exegetical Dictionary of the New Testament* 3 (1993): 157-58.
31. Stählin, "*prokoptō, ktl.*," 716; see further Lövestam, *Spiritual Wakefulness*, 30; Dunn, *Romans 9-16*, 787; Jewett, *Romans*, 821.
32. The principal proponent of the theory that Paul's eschatology developed over time was C. H. Dodd, "The Mind of Paul, II," in *New Testament Studies* (Manchester: Manchester University Press, 1953), 108-28; cf. Günther Klein, "Apokalyptische Naherwartung bei Paulus," in *Neues Testament und christliche Existenz*, ed. H. D. Betz and L. Schottroff (Tübingen: Mohr Siebeck, 1973), 241-63; Jörg Baumgarten, *Paulus und die Apokalyptik: Die Auslegung apokalyptischer Überlieferungen in den echten Paulus Briefen*

(Neukirchen-Vluyn: Neukirchener Verlag, 1975); Gerd Lüdemann, *Paulus, der Heidenapostel* (Göttingen: Vandenhoeck und Ruprecht, 1983), 1:213–71.

33. A. F. J. Klijn, "1 Thessalonians 4:13–18 and Its Background in Apocalyptic Literature," in *Paul and Paulinism*, ed. Morna D. Hooker and Stephen G. Wilson (London: Society for Promoting Christian Knowledge, 1982), 67–73; Helmut Koester, *Introduction to the New Testament*, vol. 2, *History and Literature of Early Christianity*, 2nd ed. (Berlin: de Gruyter, 2000), 120.

34. David Wenham, *The Rediscovery of Jesus' Eschatological Discourse* (Sheffield: JSOT Press, 1984), 328; C. M. Tuckett, "Synoptic Traditions in 1 Thessalonians," in *The Thessalonian Correspondence*, ed. R. F. Collins (Leuven: Leuven University Press, 1990), 171; Koester, *Introduction to the New Testament*, 2:120.

35. *Pss. Sol.* 8:18, describing the hubris with which Pompey occupied Jerusalem and desecrated the temple: "He entered with peace (*met' eirēnēs*), as a father enters his son's house; he set his feet with security (*meta asphaleias*)." The slogan, as Paul employs it, is probably adapted from the political realm, as a challenge to the "peace and security" claimed as an achievement by the Roman rulers: thus, Helmut Koester, "From Paul's Eschatology to the Apocalyptic Scheme of 2 Thessalonians," in *Paul and His World: Interpreting the New Testament in Its Context* (Minneapolis: Fortress Press, 2007), 55–69, here 62: "As a political slogan, eirēnē kai asphaleia = pax et securitas is best ascribed to the realm of Roman imperial propaganda."

36. C. L. Mearns, "Early Eschatological Development in Paul," *New Testament Studies* 27 (1980–81), 137–51; Lüdemann, *Paulus, der Heidenapostel*, 1:230, 239–40; Koester, *Introduction to the New Testament*, 2:120.

37. Joseph Plevnik, "The Parousia as Implication of Christ's Resurrection: An Exegesis of 1 Thess. 4:13–18," in *Word and Spirit: Essays in Honor of David Michael Stanley, S.J.*, ed. J. Plevnik (Willowdale: Regis College Press, 1975), 199–277; Lüdemann, *Paulus, der Heidenapostel*, 1:231–63; Brown, "Paul and the Parousia," 64–65, 67–70.

38. Koester, "From Paul's Eschatology to the Apocalyptic Scheme of 2 Thessalonians," 59, observing that "the term *parousia* is a peculiar feature" of the

Thessalonian correspondence. As has been often noted, there are no uses of the term *parousia* in reference to the second coming of Jesus in Galatians, 2 Corinthians, Philippians, or Romans: James D. G. Dunn, *The Theology of Paul the Apostle* (Grand Rapids, Mich.: Eerdmans, 1998), 307; de Boer, "Paul and Apocalyptic Eschatology," 183, 184. To be sure, Paul uses the term *parousia* in a mundane sense to describe his own "presence" or "arrival," and that of his colleagues, in 1 Corinthians 16:17; 2 Corinthians 7:6, 7; 10:10; Philippians 1:26; 2:12. Helmut Koester argues convincingly that Paul's use of the term *parousia* in reference to the second coming of Jesus in 1 Thessalonians is adapted from Roman imperial ideology. Koester, "Imperial Ideology and Paul's Eschatology in 1 Thessalonians," in *Paul and Empire: Religion and Power in Roman Imperial Society*, ed. Richard Horsley (Harrisburg: Trinity Press International, 1997), 158–66. Cf. James R. Harrison, *Paul and the Imperial Authorities at Thessalonica and Rome: A Study in the Conflict of Ideology* (Tübingen: Mohr Siebeck, 2011), 56–59.

39. Most interpreters assume that the *parousia* is implicit in talk of judgment "through Jesus Christ" in Romans 2:16, and similarly, in Romans 5:9–10, 8:29–30, 13:11: see Dunn, *Theology of Paul the Apostle*, 308. Yet, Dunn acknowledges: "In Romans 8 the failure to mention Christ's *parousia* as a fundamental feature of the climax to the salvation process remains surprising" (308). Similar assumptions are generally made about references to the "day of Messiah Jesus" in Philippians 1:6, 10.

40. A number of interpreters see a reference to Jesus's second coming in Paul's citation of Isaiah 59:20–21 (Septuagint) in Romans 11:26, in light of the future tense of the verb *hēxei* (will come): "and so all Israel will be saved, as it is written: 'Out of Zion will come the deliverer; he will turn away ungodliness from Jacob'"; see Cranfield, *Epistle to the Romans*, 2:578; Michel, *Der Brief an die Römer*, 356; Hans Hübner, *Gottes Ich und Israel: Zum Schriftgebrauch des Paulus in Römer 9–11* (Göttingen: Vandenhoeck und Ruprecht, 1984), 114; Wilckens, *Der Brief an die Römer*, 2:256–57; Dunn, *Romans 9–16*, 682; Jewett, *Romans*, 704. Other interpreters suggest that Paul was thinking of the Messiah's death and resurrection, and that the future verb (*hēxei*) should be understood as a prophecy that has already been fulfilled: see Ulrich Luz, *Das Geschichtsverständnis des Paulus* (Munich: Kaiser Ver-

lag, 1968), 294-95; Dieter Zeller, *Der Brief an die Römer*, RNT (Regensburg: Pustet, 1985), 199; Heikki Räisänen, "Römer 9-11: Analyse eines geistigen Ringes," *Aufstieg und Niedergang der römischen Welt: Geschichte und Kultur Roms im Spiegel der neueren Forschung* 2.25.4 (1987): 2920. In support of the latter interpretation may be Paul's deliberate alteration of the Septuagint text of Isaiah 59:20, substituting *ek Ziōn* ("out of Zion" or "from Zion") for *heneken Ziōn* ("for the sake of Zion"). In any case, the original reference of the Isaiah citation was to the Lord God as "the deliverer" (cf. Jub. 22:14-15), although Paul undoubtedly understood the reference in a messianic sense (cf. 1 Thess. 1:10).

41. Gerhard Delling, "*hēmera*," *Theological Dictionary of the New Testament* 2 (1964): 951-52; Jewett, *Romans*, 203, referencing Zephaniah 1:12, 15-16.

42. Schlier, *Der Römerbrief*, 257n2, referencing 4 Ezra 13:16-19; James D. G. Dunn, *Romans 1-8*, Word Biblical Commentary 38a (Dallas: Word, 1988), citing Daniel 7:21-22, 25-27; 12:1-3; *Jub.* 23:22-31; *Test. Mos.* 5-10; 1 QH 3:28-36; *Sib. Or.* 3.632-56, in support of the hypothesis that "Paul is taking over an earlier eschatological schema." Note especially Paul's use of the expression "the now time" (*ho nun kairos*) in Roman 8:18 in reference to the moment of suffering that precedes "the glory about to be revealed"; cf. Jörg Baumgarten, "*kairos*," *Exegetical Dictionary of the New Testament* 2 (1991): 233.

43. What Louis Martyn says of Paul's eschatology in Galatians is still more apposite of Romans: "The focus of Paul's apocalyptic lies not on Christ's parousia, but rather on his death." J. Louis Martyn, "Apocalyptic Antinomies in the Letter to the Galatians," *New Testament Studies* 31 (1985): 420.

44. I construe the phrase *kata kairon* with *apethanen*, as a reference to the messianic event, in agreement with Gerhard Delling, "*kairos*," *Theological Dictionary of the New Testament* 3 (1965): 460; Cranfield, *Epistle to the Romans*, 1:264; Michel, *Der Brief an die Römer*, 181; contra Jewett, *Romans*, 358, who translates "at that time."

45. Philipp Vielhauer, *Geschichte der urchristlichen Literatur* (Berlin: de Gruyter, 1975), 82; Helmut Koester, "1 Thessalonians—Experiment in Christian Writing," in *Continuity and Discontinuity in Church History: Essays Presented to George Hunston Williams*, ed. F. Forrester Church and

Timothy George (Leiden: Brill, 1979), 33–44; Koester, *Introduction to the New Testament*, 2:119.

46. Vielhauer, *Geschichte der urchristlichen Literatur*, 175; Koester, *Introduction to the New Testament*, 2:144–48.

47. For the traditional chronology, which dates the composition of 1 Thessalonians to 50 C.E. and Romans to 56 C.E., see Robert Jewett, *A Chronology of Paul's Life* (Philadelphia: Fortress Press, 1979); for the early chronology, which dates 1 Thessalonians to 41 C.E. and Romans to 56 C.E., see Lüdemann, *Paulus, der Heidenapostel*, vol. 1.

48. John T. Fitzgerald, *Cracks in an Earthen Vessel: An Examination of the Catalogues of Hardships in the Corinthian Correspondence* (Atlanta: Scholars Press, 1988); Craig S. Wansink, *Chained in Christ: The Experience and Rhetoric of Paul's Imprisonment* (Sheffield: Sheffield Academic Press, 1996); David E. Fredrickson, "Paul, Hardships, and Suffering," in *Paul in the Greco-Roman World*, ed. J. Paul Sampley (Harrisburg: Trinity Press International, 2003), 172–97; Jennifer A. Glancy, "Boasting of Beatings (2 Corinthians 11:23–25)," *Journal of Biblical Literature* 123 (2004): 99–135.

49. Manual Vogel, *Commentatio Mortis: 2 Kor 5,1–10 auf dem hintergrund anti ker ars morendi* (Göttingen: Vandenhoeck und Ruprecht, 2006); Murray J. Harris, "2 Corinthians 5:1–10: Watershed in Paul's Eschatology?," *Tyndale Bulletin* 22 (1971): 32–57.

50. Dodd, "The Mind of Paul, II," 109–18. Dodd intuited the "turning point" in Paul's eschatology "to lie somewhat about the time of II Corinthians" (116), an experience reflected in 2 Corinthians 1:8–10. Cf. A. E. Harvey, *Renewal Through Suffering: A Study of 2 Corinthians* (Edinburgh: T and T Clark, 1996).

51. Koester, "From Paul's Eschatology to the Apocalyptic Scheme of 2 Thessalonians," 66: "On the contrary, one could argue that the expectation of the nearness of these events even intensified in the later writings of Paul. Using the same terms employed in 1 Thess. 5:1–11 (*kairos ex hupnou egerthēnai, sōtēria, nux, hēmera endusasthai to hoopla tou phōtos*), Rom. 13:11–14 even radicalizes the expectation of the nearness: *nun gar egguteron hēmōn hē sōtēria ē hote episteusamen* (Rom. 13:11). Neither 1 Thessa-

lonians nor Romans was written by someone who was worried about the 'delay of the parousia.'" On whether the problem of the "delay of the parousia" was a factor in the development of Paul's eschatology, see further Dunn, *Theology of Paul the Apostle*, 310.

52. Cf. Albert Schweitzer, *The Mysticism of Paul the Apostle*, trans. William Montgomery (Baltimore: Johns Hopkins University Press, 1998), 99: "For the man of insight who dares to see things as they really are, faith ceases to be simply a faith of expectation. It takes up present certainties into itself. This invasion of a belief in the future by a belief in the present has nothing to do with the spiritualizing of the eschatological expectation; in arises in fact from the intensification of it."

53. So, Rudolf Bultmann, *The Theology of the New Testament* (New York: Scribner's, 1951), 1:278–79.

54. The "sons of God" (*huioi tou theou*) in Romans 8:19 are not the "angelic powers," as suggested by Olle Christoffersson. See Christoffersson, *The Earnest Expectation of the Creature: The Flood Tradition as Matrix of Romans 8:18–27* (Stockholm: Almqvist and Wiksell, 1990), 120–24. They are instead messianic believers, transfigured human beings: see, rightly, Schlier, *Der Römerbrief*, 260; Michel, *Der Brief an die Römer*, 266; Fitzmyer, *Romans*, 507; Jewett, *Romans*, 512. Note Paul's reference to the "sonship" of believers in Romans 8:15, 23. Paul's personification of the created world in the phrase *hē apokaradokia tēs ktiseōs* conjures a vivid image: the whole creation waits with outstretched neck for the emergence and empowerment of those human beings who will take responsibility for the redemption of the world.

6. NEIGHBOR (A')

1. H. G. Liddell and R. Scott, *Greek-English Lexicon*, revised and augmented by H. S. Jones (Oxford: Clarendon Press, 1996), 1277, s.v., *opheilō*; Walter Bauer, *A Greek-English Lexicon of the New Testament and Other Early Christian Literature*, 3rd ed., rev. and ed. Frederick William Danker (Chicago: University of Chicago Press, 2000), 743, s.v., *opheilō*; J. H. Moulton and G. Milligan, *The Vocabulary of the Greek Testament Illustrated from the Papyri and Other Non-Literary Sources* (1930; Grand Rapids, Mich.:

Eerdmans, 1985), 468, s.v., *opheilō*; Friedrich Hauck, "*opheilō, ktl.*," *Theological Dictionary of the New Testament* 5 (1967): 559–64.
2. Adolf Strobel, "Zum Verständnis von Röm 13," *Zeitschrift für die neutestamentliche Wissenschaft und die Kunde der älteren Kirche* 47 (1956): 88; Robert Jewett, *Romans: A Commentary*, Hermeneia (Minneapolis: Fortress Press, 2007), 805–6.
3. Otto Michel, *Der Brief an die Römer*, KEK 4 (Göttingen: Vandenhoeck und Ruprecht, 1978), 408.
4. Richard Saller, *Personal Patronage Under the Early Empire* (Cambridge: Cambridge University Press, 1982), 1.
5. Andrew Wallace-Hadrill, "Patronage in Roman Society: From Republic to Empire," in *Patronage in Ancient Society*, ed. A. Wallace-Hadrill (London: Routledge, 1990), 63–87, esp. 73.
6. M. I. Finley, *The Ancient Economy*, updated ed. (Berkeley: University of California Press, 1999), 64; cf. Bruce W. Frier and Dennis P. Kehoe, "Law and Economic Institutions," in *The Cambridge Economic History of the Greco-Roman World*, ed. Walter Scheidel, Ian Morris, and Richard Saller (Cambridge: Cambridge University Press, 2007), 131–32.
7. Finley, *The Ancient Economy*, 56; Wallace-Hadrill, "Patronage in Roman Society," 79–81; Anton von Premerstein, *Vom Werden und Wesen des Prinzipats* (Munich: Beck, 1937). On the structure of power in Roman society as the context for Paul's argument in Romans, see esp. Neil Elliott, *The Arrogance of Nations: Reading Romans in the Shadow of Empire* (Minneapolis: Fortress Press, 2010).
8. Philemon Comic *apud* Lucian *Laps.* 6: "First I beg good health, and second doing well, thirdly to have joy, and last to owe nobody (*opheilein mēdeni*)"; *IGRom*, 1.104: the grave inscription of a Roman woman who "lived well and owed no one anything" (*kalōs biōsasa, mēdeni mēden opheilousa*), cited by Strobel, "Zum Verständnis von Röm 13," 92; Jewett, *Romans*, 805.
9. Peter Marshall, *Enmity in Corinth: Social Conventions in Paul's Relations with the Corinthians* (Tübingen: Mohr Siebeck, 1987), 218–58, esp. 218–19, 233, 239, 252–53; L. L. Welborn, *An End to Enmity: Paul and the "Wrongdoer" of Second Corinthians* (Berlin: de Gruyter, 2011), 132–39, 368–69, 428.

10. Jewett, *Romans*, 53–70. Cf. Andrew Wallace-Hadrill, "*Domus* and *Insulae* in Rome: Families and Housefuls," in *Early Christian Families in Context: An Interdisciplinary Dialogue*, ed. Carolyn Osiek and David Balch (Grand Rapids, Mich.: Eerdmans, 2003), 3–18; Christiane Kunst, "Wohnen in der antiken Grosstadt. Zur sozialen Topographie Roms in der frühen Kaiserzeit," in *Christians as a Religious Minority in a Multicultural City: Modes of Interaction and Identity Formation in Early Imperial Rome*, ed. Jürgen Zangenberg and Michael Labahn (London: T and T Clark, 2004), 2–19.

11. For the interpretation of *ei mē* as designating an inclusive exception ("except to love one another"), rather than an antithesis ("but you ought to love one another"), see the analysis in Anton Fridrichsen, "Exegetisches zu den Paulusbriefen," *Theologische Studien und Kritiken* 102 (1930): 294–97; F. Blass and A. Debrunner, *A Greek Grammar of the New Testament and Other Early Christian Literature*, trans. and rev. R. W. Funk (Chicago: University of Chicago Press, 1961), §376, 428.3; C. E. B. Cranfield, *A Critical and Exegetical Commentary on the Epistle to the Romans*, ICC (Edinburgh: T and T Clark, 1979), 2:674; Michel, *Der Brief an die Römer*, 408n4; James D. G. Dunn, *Romans 9–16*, Word Biblical Commentary 38b (Dallas: Word, 1988), 776; Jewett, *Romans*, 806.

12. Blass and Debrunner, *Greek Grammar of the New Testament*, §399.1; Michael Thompson, *Clothed with Christ: The Example and Teaching of Jesus in Romans 12,1–15,13* (Sheffield: Sheffield Academic Press, 1991), 123; Jewett, *Romans*, 806.

13. Justin J. Meggitt, *Paul, Poverty and Survival* (Edinburgh: T and T Clark, 1998); Steven J. Friesen, "Poverty in Pauline Studies: Beyond the So-Called New Consensus," *Journal for the Study of the New Testament* 26 (2004): 323–61; Neil Elliott, "Strategies of Resistance and Hidden Transcripts in the Pauline Communities," in *Hidden Transcripts and the Arts of Resistance: Applying the Work of James C. Scott to Jesus and Paul*, ed. Richard A. Horsley (Atlanta: Society of Biblical Literature, 2004), 97–122.

14. Steven J. Friesen, "Paul and Economics: The Jerusalem Collection as an Alternative to Patronage," in *Paul Unbound: Other Perspectives on the Apostle*, ed. Mark D. Given (Peabody: Hendrickson, 2010), 27–54. Cf. L. L.

Welborn, "That There May Be Equality: The Contexts and Consequences of a Pauline Ideal," *New Testament Studies* 59 (2013): 73–90, esp. 89–90.

15. Peter Lampe, *From Paul to Valentinus: Christians at Rome in the First Two Centuries*, trans. M. Steinhauser (Minneapolis: Fortress Press, 2003), 50–56, 59, 65, 102; Lampe, "Early Christians in the City of Rome: Topographical and Social-Historical Aspects of the First Three Centuries," in *Christians as a Religious Minority in a Multicultural City: Modes of Interaction and Identity Formation in Early Imperial Rome*, ed. Jürgen Zangenberg and Michael Labahn (London: T and T Clark, 2004), 20–32.

16. Petros Vassiliadis, "The Collection Revisited," *Deltion Biblikon Meleton* 11 (1992): 42–48, esp. 44.

17. On the social status of Crispus, the former "synagogue president" (Acts 18:8), and Gaius, "the host of the whole *ekklēsia*" (Rom. 16:23), see Gerd Theissen, *The Social Setting of Pauline Christianity: Essays on Corinth* (Philadelphia: Fortress Press, 1982), 73–74; Wayne A. Meeks, *The First Urban Christians: The Social World of the Apostle Paul* (New Haven: Yale University Press, 1983), 57–58, 221n7; Peter Lampe, "Paul, Patrons, and Clients," in *Paul in the Greco-Roman World*, ed. J. Paul Sampley (Harrisburg: Trinity Press International, 2003), 496; Friesen, "Poverty in Pauline Studies," 365, observing that Gaius must have had "a larger house than the others, which makes him perhaps the wealthiest person we know of from Paul's assemblies."

18. Theissen, *The Social Setting of Pauline Christianity*, 71–73; Meggitt, *Paul, Poverty and Survival*, 75–76, 96–100; Steven J. Friesen, "Prospects for a Demography of the Pauline Mission: Corinth Among the Churches," in *Urban Religion in Roman Corinth*, ed. Daniel Schowalter and Steven Friesen (Cambridge, Mass.: Harvard University Press, 2005), 351–70; Friesen, "Poverty in Pauline Studies," 348–53.

19. Hans Dieter Betz, *2 Corinthians 8 and 9: Two Administrative Letters of the Apostle Paul*, Hermeneia (Philadelphia: Fortress Press, 1985), 43n15, 68.

20. Petros Vassiliadis, "Equality and Justice in Classical Antiquity and in Paul: The Social Implications of the Pauline Collection," *St. Vladimir's Theological Quarterly* 36 (1992): 51–59; Vassiliadis, "The Collection Revisited," *Deltion Biblikon Meleton* 11 (1992): 42–48, esp. 44; David G. Horrell, *Soli-*

darity and Difference: A Contemporary Reading of Paul's Ethics (London: T and T Clark, 2005), 239–40; L. L. Welborn, "That There May Be Equality: The Contexts and Consequences of a Pauline Ideal," *New Testament Studies* 59 (2013): 73–90.

21. Dieter Georgi, *Remembering the Poor: The History of Paul's Collection for Jerusalem* (Nashville: Abingdon, 1992), 62–67; Betz, *2 Corinthians 8 and 9*, 68–69. Cf. Michael Wolter, "*opheilō*," *Exegetical Dictionary of the New Testament* 2 (1991): 551.

22. Lampe, *From Paul to Valentinus*, 50–56, 65.

23. Ibid., 59, 63. It is impossible to determine whether the evidence of a Christian population in these districts of Rome comes from Paul's own day.

24. For *ton heteron* (the other) as the object of the participial expression *ho agapōn* (the one who loves), see Cranfield, *Epistle to the Romans*, 2:675–76; Dunn, *Romans 9–16*, 776; Jewett, *Romans*, 807–8. For the alternative construction, which takes *ton heteron* as a modifier of *nomon*, designating the Mosaic law in contrast to the Romans law, see Willi Marxsen, "Der *heteros nomos* Röm 13:8," *Theologische Zeitschrift* 11 (1955): 230–37; Franz-Josef Leenhardt, *The Epistle of Saint Paul to the Romans: A Commentary*, trans. H. Knight (London: Lutterworth, 1961), 337–38.

25. Jewett, *Romans*, 808.

26. Theodor Zahn, *Der Brief des Paulus an die Römer* (Leipzig: Deichert, 1910), 562; followed by Heinrich Schlier, *Der Römerbrief*, Herders theologischer Kommentar zum Neuen Testament 6 (Freiburg: Herder, 1977), 395; Jewett, *Romans*, 808.

27. Jacob Milgrom, *Leviticus 17–22: A New Translation with Introduction and Commentary*, Anchor Bible 3A (New York: Random House, 2000), 1652, 1654.

28. C. K. Barrett, *A Commentary on the Epistle to the Romans* (London: Black, 1957), 250; Cranfield, *Epistle to the Romans*, 2:676; Dunn, *Romans 9–16*, 776–77; Thompson, *Clothed with Christ*, 125.

29. In my view, too much attention has been paid to the utopian formula of Galatians 3:28 ("not Jew and not Greek, not slave and not free, not male and not female"), and too little attention has been devoted to the inclusive formula of 1 Corinthians 12:13 ("whether Jews or Greeks, whether

slaves or free"), which must have been the constructive basis of Paul's community foundation. Daniel Boyarin warns that Galatians 3:28 posits unity in Christ on the basis of the erasure of differences. Boyarin, *A Radical Jew: Paul and the Politics of Identity* (Berkeley: University of California Press, 1994). But see the interpretation of Galatians 3:28 in Brigitte Kahl, *Galatians Re-Imagined: Reading with the Eyes of the Vanquished* (Minneapolis: Fortress Press, 2010), 218–27.

30. Alain Badiou, *Saint Paul: The Foundation of Universalism*, trans. Ray Brassier (Stanford: Stanford University Press, 2003), 73.

31. Aristotle *Eth. Eud.* 1234b18–23, 1237a35–40, 1237b10–17, 1239a27–40; Cicero *De Amic.* 6.20, 9.31, 15.61–21.18. See further Horace *Sat.* 1.6.52–64; *Ep.* 1.7.22–24, 2.1.245–47; *Laus Pisonis* 128–37, 218; Tacitus *Dial.* 52., 6.2. Cf. Jacques Derrida, *Politics of Friendship*, trans. George Collins (London: Verso, 1997), 1–25.

32. Kenneth Reinhard, "Paul and the Political Theology of the Neighbor," *soundandsignifier.com*, UCLA Center for Jewish Studies (May 2007), 24.

33. Cranfield, *Epistle to the Romans*, 2:676–77; Schlier, *Der Römerbrief*, 395; Michel, *Der Brief an die Römer*, 410–11; Ulrich Wilckens, *Der Brief an die Römer*, 3. *Teilband Röm 12–16*, Evangelisch-katholischer Kommentar (Zürich: Benziger Verlag, 1982), 3:69–71; Thompson, *Clothed with Christ*, 125–26.

34. Jacob Taubes, *The Political Theology of Paul*, ed. Aleida Assmann with Jan Assmann, in conjunction with Horst Folkers, Wolf-Daniel Hartwich, and Christoph Schulte, trans. Dana Hollander (Stanford: Stanford University Press, 2004), 23–24; Jewett, *Romans*, 809.

35. Hans Dieter Betz, *Essays on the Sermon on the Mount*, trans. L. L. Welborn (Philadelphia: Fortress Press, 1985), 37–54, esp. 42–43; Georg Strecker, *The Sermon on the Mount: An Exegetical Commentary*, trans. O. C. Dean (Nashville: Abingdon Press, 1988), 54–55; Jewett, *Romans*, 809.

36. Heinrich Schlier, "*kephalē, anakephalaioomai*," *Theological Dictionary of the New Testament* 3 (1965): 681–82; Helmut Merklein, "*anakephalaioō*," *Exegetical Dictionary of the New Testament* 1 (1990): 82. See the discussion of "recapitulation" in Giorgio Agamben, *The Time That Remains: A*

Commentary on the Letter to the Romans, trans. Patricia Daley (Stanford: Stanford University Press, 2005), 75–77, esp. 76 on Romans 13:9–10.

37. On the determination of love by its object, see the analysis of Hannah Arendt, *Love and Saint Augustine*, ed. Joanna Vecchiarelli and Judith Chelius Stark (Chicago: University of Chicago Press, 1996), 17, 18.

38. Jacques Lacan, *The Seminar of Jacques Lacan*, book 7, *The Ethics of Psychoanalysis, 1959–1960*, trans. Dennis Porter (New York: Norton, 1992), 177–78; Lacan, *Les non-dupes errant*, December 18, 1973, as cited in Kenneth Reinhard, "Toward a Political Theology of the Neighbor," in *The Neighbor: Three Inquiries in Political Theology*, ed. Slavoj Žižek, Eric L. Santner, and Kenneth Reinhard (Chicago: University of Chicago Press, 2005), 72–73.

39. Milgrom, *Leviticus 17–22*, 1653, citing Ibn Ezra, Ramban, and Bekhor Shor. See also Hans-Peter Mathys, *Liebe deinen Nächsten wie dich selbst: Untersuchungen zum alttestamentlichen Gebot der Nächstenliebe (Lev 19,18)* (Göttingen: Vandenhoeck und Ruprecht, 1990), 4, citing Nahmanides. See the discussion in Reinhard Neudecker, "'And You Shall Love Your Neighbor as Yourself, I Am the Lord' (Lev. 19:18) in Jewish Interpretation," *Biblica* 73 (1992): 503–4; Kenneth Reinhard, "The Ethics of the Neighbor: Universalism, Particularism, Exceptionalism," *Journal of Textual Reasoning* 4 (2005), http://etext.lib.virginia.edu/journals/tr/volume4/TR_04_01eol.html.

40. David Zvi Hoffmann, *Das Buch Leviticus* (Berlin: Poppelauer, 1905), 43; Martin Buber, *Two Types of Faith* (New York: Harper Torch, 1961), 69; Edward Ullendorff, *Thought Categories in the Hebrew Bible: Studies in Rationalism, Judaism and Universalism*, ed. Raphael Loewe (London: Routledge and Kegan Paul, 1966), 277. See the discussion in Mathys, *Liebe deinen Nächsten*, 4–5.

41. On the difficulty of this text and its importance for Paul's theology, see Schlier, *Der Römerbrief*, 151–54; Michel, *Der Brief an die Römer*, 181–82; Michael Wolter, *Rechtfertigung und zukünftiges Heil: Untersuchungen zu Röm 5,1–11* (Berlin: de Gruyter, 1978), 169–76; Jewett, *Romans*, 357–62.

42. In Romans 5:3–5, "suffering" (*thlipsis*) initiates the sequence of "endurance," "character," and "hope." See also Romans 6:3–4. Cf. Walter Benjamin, "Theologico-Political Fragment," in *Reflections: Essays, Aphorisms,*

Autobiographical Writings, ed. Peter Demetz (New York: Schocken, 1986), 313: "Whereas, admittedly, the immediate Messianic intensity of the heart, of the inner individual human being, passes through misfortune, as suffering."

43. Agamben, *The Time That Remains*, 29–34.
44. This definition of "class" draws upon Karl Marx, "The Eighteenth Brumaire of Louis Bonaparte," in *Selected Works*, by Karl Marx and Friedrich Engels (London: Lawrence and Wishart, 1950), 1:302–3; cf. G. E. M. de Ste. Croix, *The Class Struggle in the Ancient Greek World: From the Archaic Age to the Arab Conquest* (Ithaca: Cornell University Press, 1981), 43. As is well known, Marx's chief work, *Capital*, breaks off just as he was about to embark upon a definition of class. On inequality and class divisions in the economy of the Roman Empire, see Walter Scheidel and Steven J. Friesen, "The Size of the Economy and the Distribution of Income in the Roman Empire," *Journal of Roman Studies* 99 (2009): 61–91; Willem M. Jongman, "The Early Roman Empire: Consumption," in *The Cambridge Economic History of the Greco-Roman World*, ed. Walter Scheidel, Ian Morris, and Richard P. Saller (Cambridge: Cambridge University Press, 2007), 592–619; Arjan Zuiderhoek, "The Concentration of Wealth and Power," in *The Politics of Munificence in the Roman Empire: Citizens, Elites and Benefactors in Asia Minor* (Cambridge: Cambridge University Press, 2009), 53–70.
45. Georg Lukács, "Class Consciousness," in *History and Class Consciousness: Studies in Marxist Dialectics*, trans. Rodney Livingstone (Cambridge, Mass.: MIT Press, 1971), 55–59; Finley, *The Ancient Economy*, 50; de Ste. Croix, *The Class Struggle in the Ancient Greek World*, 44.
46. *Sylloge Inscriptionum Graecarum*[3] 2.684; see Alexander Fuks, "Social Revolution in Dyme in 116–114 B.C.E.," in *Studies in History*, ed. D. Asheri and I. Schatzman, Scripta Hierosolymitana 23 (Jerusalem: Magnes, 1972), 21–27.
47. Appian *Bell. Civ.* 1.117–20. Cf. Joseph Vogt, *Struktur der antiken Sklavenkriege* (Wiesbaden: Akademie der Wissenschaften, 1957).
48. Tacitus *Ann.* 14.42–45; cf. de Ste. Croix, *The Class Struggle in the Ancient Greek World*, 372.
49. *Inscriptiones Graecae ad res Romanas pertinentes* 4.914; see the discussion in de Ste. Croix, *The Class Struggle in the Ancient Greek World*, 307–8. Per-

haps one should also mention the revolt of a certain Aristonicus in Asia Minor in 132/31 B.C.E., who, according to Strabo (14.1.38), "assembled a multitude of poor men and slaves whom he won over by a promise of freedom"; see J. C. Dumont, "A propos d'Aristonicos," *Eirene* 5 (1966): 189–96.

50. Fuks, "Social Revolution in Dyme," 25; de Ste. Croix, *The Class Struggle in the Ancient Greek World*, 307.
51. Appian *Bell. Civ.* 1.120. Cf. Michel Foucault, *Discipline and Punish*, trans. Alan Sheridan (London: Allen Lane, 1979), 48.
52. Tacitus *Ann.* 14.45.
53. *Sylloge Inscriptionum Graecarum*[3] 2.684; cf. de Ste. Croix, *The Class Struggle in the Ancient Greek World*, 307.
54. Pausanias *Descr. Gr.* 8.16.9.
55. Finley, *The Ancient Economy*, 44–61; Keith Hopkins, *Death and Renewal: Sociological Studies in Roman History* (Cambridge: Cambridge University Press, 1983), 2:14–20.
56. See in general, A. H. J. Greenridge, *Infamia: Its Place in Roman Public and Private Law* (Oxford: Oxford University Press, 1894); see further Thomas Wiedemann, *Emperors and Gladiators* (London: Routledge, 1992), 26.
57. Seneca *Ad Marciam* 20.3.
58. Hopkins, *Death and Renewal*, 17, 17n25, 18; Katherine E. Welch, *The Roman Amphitheatre: From Its Origins to the Colosseum* (Cambridge: Cambridge University Press, 2007), 50, 103; see also Frank Sears, *Roman Theatres: An Architectural Study* (Oxford: Oxford University Press, 2006).
59. Elizabeth Rawson, "Discrimina Ordinum: The Lex Julia Theatralis," *Papers of the British School at Rome* 55 (1987): 83–114.
60. Suetonius *Aug.* 44; Cassius Dio 55.22; 60.7; Tacitus *Ann.* 15.32; see Hopkins, *Death and Renewal*, 17n25.
61. Welch, *The Roman Amphitheatre*, 103.
62. J. Kolendo, "La repartition des places aux spectacles et la stratification sociale dans l'empire romain à propos des inscriptions sur les gradins des amphithèâtres et thèâtres," *Ktema* 6 (1981): 301–15.
63. Hopkins, *Death and Renewal*, 11, referencing Strabo 6.2.6; Martial *De Spect.* 7; cf. Donald G. Kyle, *Spectacles of Death in Ancient Rome* (London: Routledge, 1998), 185.

64. Hopkins, *Death and Renewal*, 18–19.
65. Lukács, "Class Consciousness," 55–56.
66. Ibid., 56–57.
67. Ibid., 57.
68. Ibid.
69. Text in B. E. Perry, *Aesopica* (New York: Arno Press, 1980); translation in L. W. Daly, *Aesop Without Morals* (New York: Thomas Yoseloff, 1961). On the history of the text and its transmission, see B. E. Perry, *Studies in the Text History of the Life of Aesop* (Haverford: American Philological Association, 1936), 24–26. On the date, see Daly, *Aesop Without Morals*, 22: "Internal evidence makes it likely that the Life was written by a Greek-speaking Egyptian, in Egypt, probably in the first century after Christ." For the anti-Hellenic bias and critique of the educated elite, see Daly, *Aesop Without Morals*, 20–22; John J. Winkler, *Auctor and Actor: A Narratological Reading of Apuleius's Golden Ass* (Berkeley: University of California Press, 1991), 282.
70. *Vit. Aesop.* 1, 2, 14, 18, 21, 22, 25, 30, 31, 87.
71. Indeed, Aesop is abused by his fellow-slaves who suggest that he ought to be crucified for his impudence: *Vit. Aesop.* 2, 18–19.
72. *Vit. Aesop.* 4–7. Cf. Daly, *Aesop Without Morals*, 20–22; Winkler, *Auctor and Actor*, 286.
73. *Vit. Aesop.* 4–7.
74. Ibid., 5.
75. Ibid., 6–7.
76. Lukács, "Class Consciousness," 46–82.
77. Theissen, "Social Stratification in the Corinthian Community," in *The Social Setting of Pauline Christianity*, 69–119; Meeks, *First Urban Christians*, 51–73; Dale Martin, *The Corinthian Body* (New Haven: Yale University Press, 1995); Gerd Theissen, "The Social Structure of Pauline Communities: Some Critical Remarks on J. J. Meggitt, *Paul, Poverty and Survival*," *Journal for the Study of the New Testament* 84 (2001): 65–84.
78. Betz, *2 Corinthians 8 and 9*, 43, 49–51.
79. Theissen, *The Social Setting of Pauline Christianity*, 71–73; Meggitt, *Paul, Poverty and Survival*, 75–76, 96; Wolfgang Stegemann and Ekkehard

Stegemann, *The Jesus Movement: A Social History of the First Century* (Minneapolis: Augsburg Fortress, 1999), 291-96; Friesen, "Prospects for a Demography of the Pauline Mission," 351-70, esp. 367.

80. Scott Bartchy, *Mallon Chresai: First-Century Slavery and the Interpretation of 1 Corinthians 7:21* (Missoula; Scholars Press, 1973); J. Albert Harrill, *The Manumission of Slaves in Early Christianity* (Tübingen: Mohr Siebeck, 1998), 68-128.

81. Theissen, *The Social Setting of Pauline Christianity*, 71-73; Meeks, *First Urban Christians*, 57-58, 221n7; Lampe, "Paul, Patrons, and Clients," 496; L. L. Welborn, *An End to Enmity: Paul and the "Wrongdoer" of Second Corinthiansm* (Berlin: de Gruyter, 2011), 236-50.

82. Edwin A. Judge, "Cultural Conformity and Innovation in Paul: Some Clues from Contemporary Documents," *Tyndale Bulletin* 35 (1984): 3-24, here 21; Orsolina Montevecchi, "Phoebe prostatis (Rom. 16:2)," in *Miscellania papirològica Ramon Ruca-Puig enel seuvuitantè anaiversari*, ed. S. Janeras (Barcelona: Fund S. Vives Casajuana, 1987), 205-16.

83. Lukács, "Class Consciousness," 54.

84. Agamben, *The Time That Remains*, 30; Agamben attributes the thesis that "the Marxian concept of a classless society is a secularization of the idea of messianic time" to Walter Benjamin.

85. Karl Marx, *Collected Works* (London: Lawrence and Wishart, 1975), 3:186.

86. Agamben, *The Time That Remains*, 31. Cf. Grant Poettcker, "The Messiah's Quiet Approach: Walter Benjmin's Messianic Politics," in *Paul, Philosophy, and the Theopolitical Vision: Critical Engagements with Agamben, Badiou, Žižek, and Others*, ed. Douglas Harink (Eugene, Oreg.: Cascade Books, 2010), 90-115, here 102.

87. Agamben, *The Time That Remains*, 31.

88. Ibid. Cf. Scott Bartchy, "Paul Did Not Teach 'Stay in Slavery': The Mistranslation of *Klēsis* in 1 Corinthians 7:20-21" (unpublished paper). See also Harrill, *Manumission of Slaves in Early Christianity*.

89. Agamben, *The Time That Remains*, 23.

90. Ibid., 53.

91. Ibid., 25.

92. Ibid., 57.

93. Ibid., 25, 44–58. Cf. Travis Kroeker, "Living 'As If Not': Messianic Becoming or the Practice of Nihilism," in Harink, *Paul, Philosophy, and the Theopolitical Vision*, 37–63, here 60.
94. P. Travis Kroeker, "Whither Messianic Ethics? Paul as Political Theorist," *Journal of the Society of Christian Ethics* 25 (2005): 37–58, here 51–54.
95. Kroeker, "Living 'As If Not,'" 61–62.
96. Benjamin, "Theses on the Philosophy of History," in *Illuminations*, ed. Hannah Arendt, trans. Harry Zohn (Glasgow: Fontana/Collins, 1979), 263.
97. From a conversation with Kafka as related in Max Brod, *Franz Kafka: Eine Biographie* (Prague: H. Mercy Sohn, 1937), 278.
98. Badiou, *Saint Paul*, 13–14 and passim.
99. Alain Badiou, "The Communist Hypothesis," *New Left Review* 49 (2008): 29–42, here 37.
100. Ibid., 38.
101. Ibid.
102. Ibid., 39.
103. Ibid.; Badiou, *Saint Paul*, 6–10.
104. Badiou, *Saint Paul*, 10–11.
105. Badiou, "The Communist Hypothesis," 38–39. See the insightful discussion of Badiou in Neil Elliott, "Ideological Closure in the Christ Event: A Marxist Response to Alain Badiou's Paul," in Harink, *Paul, Philosophy, and the Theopolitical Vision*, 135–54.
106. Badiou, "The Communist Hypothesis," 41.
107. Ibid.; cf. Elliott, "Ideological Closure in the Christ Event," 154.
108. See the discussion of the phrase *to de kath' heis allēlōn melē* in Blass and Debrunner, *Greek Grammar of the New Testament*, §305; Michel, *Der Brief an die Römer*, 376: "Aus *kath'hena* (1 Kor 14,31) ist das indeclinable *kath' heis* enstanden, das hart klingt"; Dunn, *Romans 9–16*, 724.
109. Badiou, *Saint Paul*, 10–14.
110. Cf. the reading of neighbor-love in Paul by Julia Kristeva, *Strangers to Ourselves*, trans. Leon S. Roudiez (New York: Columbia University Press, 1991), 77–83: the strangeness of the other is absorbed into a new, singular universality through identification with Christ.
111. On the ethics of hospitality between the "strong" and the "weak" in the Roman communities addressed by Paul, see Mark Reasoner, *The Strong*

and the Weak: Romans 14:1—15:13 in Context (Cambridge: Cambridge University Press, 1999); Jewett, Romans, 829–99.
112. Badiou, "The Communist Hypothesis," 37. Or, to use Paul's own expression, a "making new of the mind" (anakaiōsis tou noos) which brings about "transformation" (morphousthai), in place of conformity to this world (Rom. 12:2).
113. See the discussion of the various political interpretations of Paul's vision of a messianic community by Agamben, The Time That Remains, 31–33. Agamben outlines three alternatives: revolution without revolt (Stirner), revolution coincident with revolt (Marx, elaborated by Lukács), revolution indistinguishable from revolt (Benjamin, elaborated by Taubes).
114. Similarly, Agamben, The Time That Remains, 33.
115. Helmut Koester, Introduction to the New Testament, vol. 2, History and Literature of Early Christianity (Berlin: de Gruyter, 1987), 142. A number of scholars have proposed that Romans 13:1–7 is an interpolation by a redactor: Alexander Pallis, To the Romans: A Commentary (Liverpool: Liverpool Booksellers, 1920), 141; Christian Eggenberger, "Der Sinn der Argumentation in Röm 13,2–5," Kirchenblatt für die reformierte Schweiz 101 (1945): 242–45; Ernst Barnikol, "Römer 13: Der nichtpaulinische Ursprung der absoluten Obrigkeitsbejahung in Röm 13,1–7," in Studien zum Neuen Testament und zur Patristik: Erich Klostermann zum 90. Geburtstag dargebracht (Berlin: Akademie Verlag, 1961), 65–133; James Kallas, "Romans XIII:1–7: An Interpolation," New Testament Studies 11 (1964–65): 365–74; J. C. O'Neill, Paul's Letter to the Romans (London: Penguin, 1975), 207–10; Winsome Munro, Authority in Paul and Peter (Cambridge: Cambridge University Press, 1983), 56–67, 79; Walter Schmithals, Der Römerbrief: Ein Kommentar (Gütersloh: Mohn, 1988), 191–97. The reasons offered in support of the proposal seem compelling: (1) 12:21 finds its continuation in 13:8 (mēdeni kakon [12:17] . . . mē nikō [12:21] . . . mēdeni mēden opheilete [13:8]); by contrast, the transition from 12:21 to 13:1 is abrupt, lacking a conjunction, and shifting from the second-person admonitions of 12:9–21 to the third-person style of 13:1ff.; (2) the vocabulary of 13:1–7 is not especially Pauline: diatagē (ordinance) and antitassō (oppose, resist) are hapax legomena within the Pauline corpus; (3) the attitude of submission to the "governing authorities" in 13:1–2 stands in contrast to the critical

attitude toward the "rulers of this age" exhibited in 1 Corinthians 12:8. In consequence, even scholars who do not regard Romans 13:1–7 as an interpolation by a redactor recognize that it is an "independent insertion" (*selbständige Einlage*) alien to its present context: Michel, *Der Brief an die Römer*, 393–94; see also Martin Dibelius, "Rom und die Christen im ersten Jahrhundert," in *Botschaft und Geschichte: Gesammelte Aufsätze* (Tübingen: Mohr Siebeck, 1953), 2:177–228, here 182; Ernst Käsemann, *Commentary on Romans*, trans. G. W. Bromiley (Grand Rapids, Mich.: Eerdmans, 1980), 352; Wilckens, *Der Brief an die Römer*, 3:30. Among attempts to make the diatribe of Romans 13:1–7 comprehensible as authentically Pauline in the context of Romans 12:1—13:14, one may mention: Ernst Bammel, "Romans 13," in *Jesus in the Politics of His Day*, ed. E. Bammel and C. F. D. Moule (Cambridge: Cambridge University Press, 1984), 365–83; J. Friedrich, W. Pöhlmann, and P. Stühlmacher, "Zur historischen Situation und Intention von Röm 13,1–7," *Zeitschrift für Theologie und Kirche* 73 (1986): 131–66; Neil Elliott, "Romans 13:1–7 in the Context of Imperial Propaganda," in *Paul and Empire: Religion and Power in Roman Imperial Society*, ed. Richard A. Horsley (Harrisburg: Trinity Press International, 1997), 184–204; James R. Harrison, "Did Paul Found a New Concept of State?," in *Paul and the Imperial Authorities at Thessalonica and Rome: A Study in the Conflict of Ideology* (Tübingen: Mohr Siebeck, 2011), 271–323.

116. For example, Josephus B.J. 2.140; 4.175. Cf. Barnikol, "Römer 13," 74–80; on the language of Hellenistic-Jewish paraenesis, see Dibelius, "Rom und die Christen," 183–84; Gerhard Delling, Römer 13:1–7 innerhalb der Briefe des Neuen Testaments (Berlin: Evangelische Verlagsanstalt, 1962), 56–57; Delling, "hupotassō," *Theological Dictionary of the New Testament* 8 (1972): 39–40; Wolfgang Schrage, "Römer 13," in *Die Christen und der Staat nach dem Neuen Testament* (Gütersloh: Mohn, 1975), 64; W. C. van Unnik, "Lob und Strafe durch Obrigkeit: Hellenistisches zu Röm 13,3–4," in *Jesus und Paulus: Festschrift für Werner Georg Kümmel zum 70. Geburtstag*, ed. E. Earle Ellis and E. Grässer (Göttingen: Vandenhoeck und Ruprecht, 1975), 334–43; Michel, "Zur Eigenart der Tradition Röm 13,1–7," in *Der Brief an die Römer*, 395–97.

117. Contrast the dearth of monographs on Romans 13:8–10 or 13:11–14 with the number and influence of works devoted to Romans 13:1–7 in the his-

tory of interpretation; cf. O'Neill, *Paul's Letter to the Romans*, 209; Neil Elliott, *Liberating Paul: The Justice of God and the Politics of the Apostle* (Maryknoll: Orbis Books, 1994), 13–19.

118. De Ste. Croix, *The Class Struggle in the Ancient Greek World*, 432–33, 439.

7. CODA

1. Giorgio Agamben, *The Highest Poverty: Monastic Rules and Form-of-Life* (Stanford: Stanford University Press, 2013).
2. Taylor Branch, *Parting the Waters: America in the King Years, 1954–63* (New York: Simon and Schuster, 1988); Branch, *Pillar of Fire: America in the King Years, 1963–65* (New York: Simon and Schuster, 1998); Branch, *At Canaan's Edge: America in the King Years, 1965–68* (New York: Simon and Schuster, 2006).
3. Giorgio Agamben, *The Church and the Kingdom*, trans. Leland de la Durantaye (London: Seagull Books, 2012).
4. Ibid., 41.
5. Ibid.
6. L. L. Welborn, "That There May Be Equality: The Contexts and Consequences of a Pauline Ideal," *New Testament Studies* 59 (2013): 73–90, esp. 74.

INDEX

Agamben, Giorgio, xi, xii, xv, 8, 14–17, 65–67, 71, 121n82, 123n113
agape, 59–60,
Akiba, 1
Arendt, Hannah, 117n37
awakening, 23–30, 37–43, 49, 69

Badiou, Alain, xi, xii, 8, 67–68
Benjamin, Walter, vii, xiii, xiv, 117–18n42
Benveniste, Émil, 19
biopolitics, xii
Boyarin, Daniel, 116n29
Brown, Alexandra R., 104–5n13
Bultmann, Rudolf, 88n59

Caligula, 26, 93n32
chronos, 16–17, 19
class consciousness, 60–69, 118n44, 118–19n49, 119n62, 121n82
Cleitophon (Pseudo-Plato), 37–38, 97n7
Crossan, John Dominic, 18

Derrida, Jacques, 116n31
Dodd, C. H., 18

Epictetus, 37–38

Freud, Sigmund, 2–5
Francis of Assisi, 71

Guillaume, Gustav, 14–15

Heidegger, Martin, 78n52
heteros, 58, 69
Hillel, 1

Jewett, Robert, 80n3, 80n4

Kafka, Franz, 67
Kahl, Brigitte, 116n29
kairos, xiv, 7, 11–21, 45–53, 80n4, 109n42
kenōsis, 2, 75n12
kingdom of God, 9, 17–20, 86n50
klēsis, 2, 61, 66

Koester, Helmut, 70
Kristeva, Julia, 8, 122n110

Lacan, Jacques, 5, 68, 117n38
Laplanche, Jean, 5
Lenin, Nikolai, xi, 67
Levinas, Emmanuel, 6–7
Leviticus, 1–3, 58–60
Life of Aesop, 63–64, 120n69, 120n70, 120n71, 120n72
Lukács, Georg, 63, 65

Marx, Karl, 65–66, 118n44, 123n113
mutualism, 56–57

Nero, xii, xiii, 63, 95n48
nomos, 58–59
nun kairos, xv, 8, 13, 14–15, 17, 20

parousia, xvi, 15, 16, 51, 98n19, 107–8n38, 108n39, 109n40
patronage, 55–57
Poimandres, 37–38
Psalms of Solomon, 9, 12, 42, 51, 107n35

Q, the Sayings Gospel, 17–18, 19, 86–87n51, 89n66

Reinhard, Kenneth, xi, 4–5
revolution, 70, 123n113
Romans 13:1–7, 70, 123–24n115, 124n116
Rosenzweig, Franz, 5–6

Santner, Eric, xi, 4, 5–6
Schlier, Heinrich, 80n3
Schweitzer, Albert, 18, 84–85n25, 111n52
Seneca, 23–27, 29–30, 42, 90n3, 94n42
sleep, 23–30, 49–50, 69, 96n61, 105–6n19
Spivak, Gayatri, 8
state of exception, xii
sublation, 3

Tacitus, 93n26, 94n42
Taubes, Jacob, xi, 2–4, 8, 9, 74–75n8, 78n50, 123n113
Testament of Levi, 9, 12
Testament of Reuben, 89n1

Weiss, Johannes, 18

Žižek, Slavoj, xi, 4, 5, 6–7

INSURRECTIONS: CRITICAL STUDIES IN RELIGION, POLITICS, AND CULTURE
Slavoj Žižek, Clayton Crockett, Creston Davis, Jeffrey W. Robbins, Editors

After the Death of God, John D. Caputo and Gianni Vattimo, edited by Jeffrey W. Robbins

The Politics of Postsecular Religion: Mourning Secular Futures, Ananda Abeysekara

Nietzsche and Levinas: "After the Death of a Certain God," edited by Jill Stauffer and Bettina Bergo

Strange Wonder: The Closure of Metaphysics and the Opening of Awe, Mary-Jane Rubenstein

Religion and the Specter of the West: Sikhism, India, Postcoloniality, and the Politics of Translation, Arvind Mandair

Plasticity at the Dusk of Writing: Dialectic, Destruction, Deconstruction, Catherine Malabou

Anatheism: Returning to God After God, Richard Kearney

Rage and Time: A Psychopolitical Investigation, Peter Sloterdijk

Radical Political Theology: Religion and Politics After Liberalism, Clayton Crockett

Radical Democracy and Political Theology, Jeffrey W. Robbins

Hegel and the Infinite: Religion, Politics, and Dialectic, edited by Slavoj Žižek, Clayton Crockett, and Creston Davis

What Does a Jew Want? On Binationalism and Other Specters, Udi Aloni

A Radical Philosophy of Saint Paul, Stanislas Breton, edited by Ward Blanton, translated by Joseph N. Ballan

Hermeneutic Communism: From Heidegger to Marx, Gianni Vattimo and Santiago Zabala

Deleuze Beyond Badiou: Ontology, Multiplicity, and Event, Clayton Crockett

Self and Emotional Life: Philosophy, Psychoanalysis, and Neuroscience, Adrian Johnston and Catherine Malabou

The Incident at Antioch: A Tragedy in Three Acts / L'Incident d'Antioche: Tragédie en trois actes, Alain Badiou, translated by Susan Spitzer

Philosophical Temperaments: From Plato to Foucault, Peter Sloterdijk

To Carl Schmitt: Letters and Reflections, Jacob Taubes, translated by Keith Tribe

Encountering Religion: Responsibility and Criticism After Secularism, Tyler Roberts

Spinoza for Our Time: Politics and Postmodernity, Antonio Negri, translated by William McCuaig

Factory of Strategy: Thirty-three Lessons on Lenin, Antonio Negri, translated by Arianna Bove

Cut of the Real: Subjectivity in Poststructuralism Philosophy, Katerina Kolozova

A Materialism for the Masses: Saint Paul and the Philosophy of Undying Life, Ward Blanton

Our Broad Present: Time and Contemporary Culture, Hans Ulrich Gumbrecht

Wrestling with the Angel: Experiments in Symbolic Life, Tracy McNulty

Cloud of the Impossible: Negative Theology and Planetary Entanglements, Catherine Keller

What Does Europe Want? The Union and Its Discontents, Slavoj Žižek and Srecko Horvat